In the Beginning God Created . . .

"I see this book as scientific common sense based on solid Christian values. Frank but not obscene. Reverent but not prudish," comments author James C. Hefley.

In an age when the morning paper brings news of galaxies newly visible and man's conquest of the moon, and magazines carry articles on co-ed dorms and youth communes, it's easy to overreact as the realization dawns that every day is different—not just a new day, but a different day—changed by advances in technology, science, and knowledge.

We, the people, awaken to the changes of each different day, and find ourselves marveling with a tumult of thoughts: Science is fantastic—imagine pre-programmed babies tailor made to your specifications. What if an evil man develops a super race? A hereditary disease doesn't have to be passed on to my children? A do-it-yourself wedding ceremony— the idea!

On and on it goes, and the Christian reads and assimilates. He fits the change in God's world into harmony with the Bible and his faith, and his faith changes. It grows and expands—because an all-wise, all powerful God is not threatened by the advances of His Creation. We must stand in awe in the presence of Jehovah God, for our minds cannot comprehend or our words proclaim such Total Greatness.

SEX
SENSE AND NONSENSE

**What the Bible Does and
Doesn't Say About Sex**

JAMES C. HEFLEY

DAVID C. COOK PUBLISHING CO.
Elgin, Illinois 60120

SEX SENSE AND NONSENSE
What the Bible Does and Doesn't Say About Sex

Published for the David C. Cook Publishing Co. by
Pyramid Publications

First printing, June 1971

Copyright © 1971 by David C. Cook Publishing Co.

Library of Congress Catalog Card Number: 71-147213

Quotations from the NEW TESTAMENT IN MODERN
ENGLISH, by J. B. Phillips, are used by
permission of The Macmillan Company.
                    © J. B. PHILLIPS 1958
THE GOSPELS © The Macmillan Company 1952, 1957,
THE YOUNG CHURCH IN ACTION
© The Macmillan Company 1955
LETTERS TO YOUNG CHURCHES
© The Macmillan Company 1947, 1957,
THE BOOK OF REVELATION
© The Macmillan Company 1957

Printed in the United States of America

DAVID C. COOK PUBLISHING CO.
Elgin, Illinois 60120, U.S.A.

CONTENTS

APPRECIATIONS

First and foremost, I thank my wife Marti for the companionship and communion which has provided the emotional and spiritual base for writing this book. She has also edited the manuscript to "see that women are fairly represented." Unfortunately, it seems that most sex books are written by men only.

Secondly, I thank the David C. Cook Publishing Co. for its willingness to publish this book.

Thirdly, I thank Byron T. Scott, editor of *Today's Health* (published by the American Medical Association), for inviting me to participate in a seminar on "Sex and the Science Writer" at the University of Chicago. Much of the factual information contained herein came out of that meeting.

However, the Bible was my principal source book, and I would recommend it as containing the best principles governing sexual relationships. I say "principles" because the Bible is not a marriage manual, any more than it is a geology textbook.

Besides the Bible I consulted a wide range of literature on sex. As Marti warned vistors while I was at work: "Don't jump to the wrong conclusion when you see the books on my husband's desk. He isn't obsessed with sex—just writing about it."

Why This Book?

An aging, world-famous medical researcher sighed as he said, tongue-in-cheek, "Remember the good old days when the air was clean and sex was dirty?"

His audience of about 25 science and medical writers first laughed, then looked chagrined. Health authorities had been telling them about the dramatic rise of venereal disease and unwed adolescent pregnancies.

"We have more sex education, better and more available contraceptives, and the means to cure venereal disease fast," he said. "Why the problems are greater than ever before is a puzzle to all of us."

As the only religion writer at the University of Chicago symposium, I sensed a frustration among the participants. Dr. Morris Fishbein, a distinguished medical writer, told our group, "I can remember when a newspaper simply would not print either the words *gonorrhea* or *syphilis*. How times have changed!"

At this symposium, titled "Sex and the Science Writer," the hard facts of America's sexual crisis were put before us. One scientist gloomily compared the present crisis with the lack of sexual controls in Rome just before the Empire's fall.

Almost everybody seems to be talking about sex except Christians. A few books and articles have appeared, but pastors don't preach on the subject and most Sunday school teachers are too embarrassed to talk about it. When some of us do say the word it comes out sounding like venereal disease. About the only evidence of sex in the church is the nursery.

We can't pretend any longer that sex doesn't exist. Advertising is sex-oriented. Commercial publishers don't think novels will sell without explicit sexual dialogue and description that would have been taboo even in a doctor's office 25 years ago. American movies are so sex-filled that French censors must sometimes apply the scissors. Popular songs go further than mere suggestion. Wife-swapping clubs, nude parties, and free-love communes have become so ordinary that they seldom make headlines. Hugh Hefner makes millions in his "Playboy World." Some theologians pontificate that sex outside of marriage may be the most loving thing to do in certain circumstances. Americans are so confused, said humorist James Thurber, that "they can't tell love from sex, lust, Snow White, or Ever After."

We are reminded *too often* that our present bewilderment is a reaction to Puritanism, Victorianism, and monasticism. "The church told us that sex was evil for 19 centuries," a swinger says. "We've discovered that it's fun."

So while some church leaders keep silent and others talk loftily about "responsible liberty" and "walking in the spirit," many youths are losing control of a noble gift of God. It's time for some straight, honest talk from a Christian perspective. It's time to say out in the open that Christians must develop a new Bible-based concept of sex.

It's time for the Bible searchlight to be turned on modern perversions that range from saying "sex is everything" to "sex is nothing." It's time that the big "sex fraud" perpetrated by greedy magazine publishers, movie makers, fashion designers, and pornographers be exposed.

It's time that sex education becomes a normal part

8

of growing up, and that open and natural conversation replaces embarrassed and hushed phrases.

A noted evangelist, who has been talking more about sex lately, was once asked by a student, "What do you think about sex?" The evangelist replied, "I think it's very important. Without sex I wouldn't be here."

Sex is important for reasons other than procreation, as we shall see. As one wag put it, "Sex is not the only important thing in the world, but it's way ahead of whatever is in second place."

> —JAMES C. HEFLEY, *former evangelical pastor, now a free-lance Christian journalist.*

CHAPTER ONE

Why Boys Are Boys and Girls Are Girls

"I praise Thee because I have been fearfully and wonderfully made; marvelous is Thy workmanship."[1]

David's tribute to his creator is especially appropriate to the sexual development of the human body. It is fearful—but wonderful.

Sex comes from the Latin *sexus*, meaning division. All living creatures are divided by sex. The sex of a baby is determined by the father. If the sperm carries an X chromosome, the child will be a girl. If it carries a Y, the child will be a boy. A medical researcher only recently peered through a revolutionary new microscope and saw that "boy" sperms are round-headed and "girl" sperms oval-shaped.

No Need to Guess

No microscope is needed at birth for a person to tell the sex of the child. A boy comes equipped with a tiny *penis* which for the first few years of his life will be useful only for passing urine. Underneath the penis and hanging between the tiny legs is a small skin sac called the *scrotum*. It contains the male sex glands, the *testes*, also called *testicles*, in which the boy's sperm will later be manufactured.

Behind each testicle is a storage room called the *epididymis*—actually a collection of tiny tubes— where the sperm cells will mature as they pass through. From storage, these cells will travel through a long flexible tube toward two small pouches, called *seminal vesicles*, on the back of the prostate gland.

[1]Psalm 139: 14, *New Berkeley Version.*

The prostate will secrete a slippery liquid that mixes with the sperm to produce *semen*, a Latin word meaning "seed." When the boy reaches *puberty* (from the Latin *puber*—an adult), stimulation may result in semen being discharged through the penis.

The girl's delicately balanced sexual system is beautifully designed to complement the boy's. Her *vagina* is a passage opening from outside the body and connecting the *uterus* or womb. The vagina opens between the legs where it is protected by folds of skin and flesh known as the *vulva* (from the Latin: *volva* —a covering). Where the inner folds of the vulva come together near the upper end of the vagina there is a small tip called the *clitoris* which is similar to the male penis. The vagina's opening may be partly closed by a thick membrane, which is called the *hymen*.

The female's egg cells, *ova*, are stored in two organs called *ovaries*, one on each side of the uterus. At birth, the ovaries of a girl baby already contain thousands of egg cells. They will lie undeveloped until the girl reaches puberty and is physiologically able to conceive and give birth.

The average age of puberty in girls is earlier than it once was. Dr. Joseph R. Swartout, a professor of obstetrics and gynecology at the University of Chicago Medical School, notes that 40 years ago puberty came at an average age of 14.7 years; today it begins at 11.3 years. This, he thinks, is one reason for the increasing number of illegitimate births among younger girls.

Growing Signs

Just before puberty the boy or girl's pituitary gland, located beneath the brain, produces a hormone that causes the sex glands in the girl's ovaries and in the boy's testicles to begin producing their own hormones. These hormones signal the pituitary gland to produce less of the growth hormone. Thus a youth's rate of growth in height slows not long after he becomes sexually mature.

The hormones in the female ovaries and the male testes help to bring about certain "secondary sexual characteristics" in the adolescent.

The girl begins to look more like a woman. Her hips round out and become broader, and her breasts enlarge. Hair grows under her arms and in a triangular area on and around her vulva.

Her new curves reveal a functional preparation for motherhood. The widening of her hips allows more body room for her elastic uterus to expand and accommodate the growth of a baby. The developing breasts are preparing her to nurse her young.

The boy's body becomes more masculine. His frame enlarges and his shoulders widen. Hair appears and thickens first in his pubic region, then under his arms. Hair may thicken on the chest and other parts of the body. He begins thinking about shaving.

Both the girl's and the boy's voices show change. The girl's voice becomes richer and fuller. Change in the boy's voice is more noticeable as he "squeaks" into manhood.

Why a Girl Has Periods

At puberty the girl's reproductive organs begin a process that is repeated every 28 days or so for the next 30 to 40 years. At the beginning of each "period," a ripe egg, *ovum* (singular of *ova*), is released by one of her two ovaries. (The ovaries do not necessarily take turns.) The egg, only about 1/200th of an inch long, moves into the *Fallopian tube*—also called the *oviduct*—and starts toward the uterus. In perfect timing, the uterus has prepared a nourishing soft bed of tiny, delicate blood vessels for the egg to grow in.

The miracle of reproduction begins when the egg cell is fertilized by a male sperm cell. Only the head of one sperm cell can enter the egg cell. The sperm

13

head enlarges so that each of the 23 chromosomes it carries may unite with the corresponding 23 chromosomes in the egg cell. At this moment all the hereditary features of the person are present in miniature in this fusion. The color of the eyes and hair, the size of the feet, the shape of the nose have all been determined.

Should the female egg not be fertilized, it lives for only about 12 hours after entering the Fallopian tube. It then breaks up and is absorbed into the body. No longer needed, the growth "bed" in the uterus (lining, blood, and blood vessels) is discarded through the vagina and out of the body. This every-four-weeks event is called *menstruation* and lasts from three to seven days.

About two weeks after menstruation another egg cell ripens in an ovary and is released in another two weeks. Then the whole cycle starts all over again.

When Can a Boy Become a Father?

Typically, a boy reaches puberty about a year later than a girl. Three or four months after his first pubic hair appears, the boy's penis, under sexual excitement of mind or body, may fill with blood, become firm and erect, and ejaculate semen. However, many boys have erections and "dry" ejaculations—without semen— long before. Puberty—the time when the testes begin producing sperm cells—is revealed when semen is ejaculated. From this time on a boy is capable of fatherhood.

The first tell-tale evidence that a boy has reached puberty may be a wet spot in his bed. He may have many other "seminal emissions" or "wet dreams" in the future, although some boys do not have them. A boy may experience erection and ejaculation in a variety of other situations. Sometimes the cause may be physical, as when the bladder is full, or when climbing a tree. Or it may happen when he is sexually

14

stirred—reading, watching television, daydreaming about sex, masturbating (self-stimulation of the sex organ), or for no apparent reason at all.

An average young man may have four to five hundred million sperm cells in a teaspoonful of semen. Viewed under a powerful microscope, a male sperm cell looks a little like a tadpole, with a large head at one end and an active tail. The first researchers who viewed them in the Middle Ages thought they were "little people"!

Sperm cells (also called *spermatozoa*) are ejaculated through a tube, known as the *urethra*, which runs the entire length of the penis. The urethra is also the outlet for urine from the bladder. Sperm and urine do not normally pass through at the same time because the opening from the bladder into the urethra closes when the sperm cells are thrust out.

The sperm cells reach the urethra in a complex, round-about way. They grow in hundreds of very small, coiled tubes that are in each testis. All of these tubes open into a larger tube, through which the sperm cells leave.

The larger tube forms a mass of coils behind the testes and in the scrotum where the sperm cells may remain stored temporarily. The tube straightens and rises to open into the urethra. Along the way, the tube connects with glands which help to produce the whitish fluid in which the sperm cells are discharged from the penis. This is the *semen.*

No Obscenity in the Sex Act

In the love-making which naturally precedes "intercourse" (also called "mating," "coitus," "making love," "having sex," "having relations") the minds and bodies of husband and wife prepare for mating.

Blood flows at a faster rate to the sex organs. The husband's penis becomes erect and his wife's vagina becomes moist and soft. In a loving, private, and deeply personal relationship, the husband's organ enters his wife's vagina easily and they communicate their love for each other in an intimate and joyous way.

The membrane called the hymen, which partly covers the vagina, may be broken the first time the wife has intercourse with her husband. We say "may" because it is now known that the thickness of the hymen varies or it may be incomplete at birth. A broken hymen is not necessarily the sign of previous sexual experience.

The husband's love for his wife moves him to hold back his "climax" and wait for his mate's response. A man is almost always aroused more quickly than a woman.

The peak of sexual pleasure for them both is orgasm. For the husband this is when his semen is ejaculated inside his wife's vagina in a series of quick spurts near the neck of the uterus. For the woman, orgasm is a series of muscular contractions of the walls of the vagina. After their mutual climax, which may not occur at the same moment, a couple that has given their deepest love will relax in deep happiness and peace.

When no contraceptive or preventive is used, the husband's sperm cells swim along into the uterus and then into the Fallopian tubes. If an egg cell is present in one of the tubes at this time, conception may occur. The wife's egg is present for only a part of the month and it is difficult to predict exactly when this is. Obviously, the sperm cells do not find an egg cell during every mating.

Some proponents of "free love" (sex with anyone of mutual choosing) argue that the sex drive is just a powerful hunger. They see little difference in attitude between the urge for sex and the desire for food. The celebrated sex researchers Masters and Johnson say that the sexual function is the only natural physical function that can be governed by man instead of by natural laws. Breathing, digesting, and discharging waste cannot be influenced by ideas.

Sexual function and response can be elevated to a sublime plan. When God said that man is to be "one flesh,"[2] in marriage, He meant far more than a physical union. Animals may mate, but only man and woman can know the beautiful sexual expression which God intended.

Penises and vaginas can't make love; only people can. Sex is not just something a man does to a woman. Sex is the primary form of interpersonal communion between two persons who are uniquely different and complementary to each other.

No Unisex in the Beginning

An ancient Greek myth says that the earth was once populated by beings who were half-man and half-woman. Each person was both masculine and feminine and thereby perfect and complete. These two-sex people became proud and rebelled against the gods. Zeus responded in anger and split each one in half, scattering the halves over the earth. Ever since, according to the legend, each half has been seeking its other for completion and fulfillment.

God didn't consult the fashion designers of the new unisex outfits when "male and female created he them."[3] A person's sexuality is God-given. Sexuality is everything that makes a man masculine and a woman feminine. No one can properly understand and appreciate sex without recognizing basic differences between sexes.

Not only are the sex organs different, but the male and female skeletons are not the same. A man may even undergo "sex surgery" and proclaim himself a woman, yet when his skeleton is dug up he will be

[2]Genesis 2: 24.
[3]Genesis 1: 27.

17

identified as a man. A man is a man and a woman is a woman. And as the Frenchman would say, "*Viva la différence!*"

Freud once said, "After 30 years of studying them, I ask myself, 'What is it that women want?'" Other men have found women equally puzzling. Every husband has said at one time or another, "I'll never understand women."

It is impossible to compare the sexes, but we can make some general observations.

A woman's emotional cycle has more ups and downs than a man's. She can be "up in the clouds" or "down in the dumps" for what may seem a silly reason to a man.

A woman is more "personal" than a man. A man tends to be more concerned with matter and mind, business and facts. A woman has a deeper interest in persons and feelings. She thinks both with her heart and mind. She responds with her emotions and her feelings to something which a man may see only in cold mechanical terms. For example, my wife and I were discussing the effects of President John Kennedy's assassination while we were still stunned by the news.

"How will the country react?" I said. "Will there be more violence? What will other nations think of us now?"

Marti frowned. "All you're concerned about are the political and international complications. What worries me is who's going to tell those two little children that their daddy is dead."

A woman is warm and affectionate. She may greet a friend with a hug while a man will make do with a handshake. She is usually more sympathetic, tender, and interested in another person's feelings. She wants to give help, encouragement, and support. She has a capacity for love and tenderness which a man may not consider it manly to have.

18

A century ago Dr. William Acton—then considered the greatest authority on sex—declared, "Most women, happily for them and happily for society, are not much troubled with sexual feeling of any kind." We now know this is not true. A woman does feel the need for a man—but for far more than just sex. In contrast a man may think more on the biological level.

Higher than Animals

A woman wants love, acceptance, security, strength, and—yes—sometimes even dominance from a man. She wants to give herself to him, but only in an atmosphere of love and mutual commitment. She wants sex in the context of intimate love, a closeness which makes two hearts beat as one, a fusion of emotions and feelings in a spiritual unity.

Animals usually mate only when the female is in "heat"—that is, when the female has released an egg cell and is ready to be made pregnant. The female animal then gives forth a certain scent to arouse the male and signal that she is ready for mating.

Humans live on a higher plane. The Lord has a larger purpose for human sex than mere procreation. It is the ultimate expression of love.

The woman is not always ready for sex. Her body does not give forth a special scent. She seldom knows when she has an egg ready to be fertilized. She is influenced by mood, feeling, atmosphere, circumstances, and most of all by the attitude of her husband.

The husband is more influenced by his glands than his heart. He is more easily and quickly aroused. Unless he applies self-control he can become a brute. No wife likes to be "used" by her husband. Marriage is not a license for selfish sex.

Meaningful sex always comes wrapped in the cocoon of love. Mere sex by itself is not really "making love" though it is often erroneously called so. In an old Clark Gable movie Gene Tierney as a Russian ballerina looks wide-eyed at Gable and asks, "You have loved many?" Gable, playing the role of an American correspondent, replies, "Made love, sure. Loved—none."

The greatest pleasure in sexual intercourse is not the contact of two skins, but the mutual giving of two persons to each other in genuine affection. "Orgasm" then becomes not just the release of sexual energy, but the fullest expression of personality in precious love.

Sex Is Social

Sex also relates to loved ones and friends. A girl's parents certainly have the right to know that she is not being exploited. Sex relates to the community and country. Sexual promiscuity has certainly been a contributing factor in the decadence of past civilizations, notably the Roman Empire.

Most of all, sex relates to the Creator, who made possible the highest expression of intimacy between man and woman.

CHAPTER TWO

Old Testament: What It Says About Sex

"Male and female created he them."[1]

The first pair was neither two men nor two women, but a man and a woman. Birds and bees and other creatures of both sexes were already thriving. Only after making man and woman did God say, "Very good."[2] His first commandment was "Be fruitful, and multiply, and replenish the earth. . . ."[3]

God Chose Sex

God intended that *homo sapiens* follow the method He had instituted among the lesser creation and continue the human species through sexual union. The Creator chose not to follow the plan later preferred by Martin Luther. The Reformer, reacting to the sexual immorality of high churchmen, said, "Had God consulted me in the matter, I should have advised Him to continue the generation of the species by fashioning human beings out of clay as Adam was made."

Sex Without Hangups

Genesis 2 gives the divine intent of sex in more detail. "It is not good that the man should be alone . . . Therefore shall a man leave his father and his mother, and shall cleave unto his wife: and they shall be one flesh."[4] Note the order: "leave," "cleave," "be one flesh."

[1]Genesis 1: 27.
[2]Genesis 1: 31.
[3]Genesis 1: 28.
[4]Genesis 2: 18, 24.

21

"One flesh" (implying in the Hebrew "one person") expresses the essence of intimate love. More than mere physical union which animals can attain, it is the merging of two personalities. Intimacy becomes unity. Feelings are fused. Two hearts beat as one.

"They were both naked, the man and his wife, and were not ashamed."[5] They had no hangups, no frustrations, no inhibitions, and no guilt. They were in perfect harmony. Thus in Scripture—not in a marriage manual or a movie—is expressed the perfect ideal of sexual love.

Was Sexual Intercourse the Original Sin?

The first honeymoon was spoiled by sin. Eve first, then Adam, yielded to the temptation to eat the forbidden, to know as much as God, to disobey the Creator. They surrendered not to sexual desire, but to pride and rebellion. Their sin, disobedience to God's command, brought knowledge and guilt and shame. For the first time they became self-conscious of their nakedness and covered their sexual organs with fig leaves.

The woman sinned first and on her were pronounced the first penalties. "To the woman He said: I will greatly increase your pregnancy-troubles; you will suffer birth-pangs; yet, you will be drawn to your husband and he will dominate you."[6] Ever since, man has dominated woman, especially in Bible lands. Despite recurring cries for equality and independence, woman has continued to desire the one who dominates her.

Did God Sanction Polygamy?

Monogamy—one man and one woman—was clearly the divine ideal in the beginning. One man and two

[5] Genesis 2: 25.
[6] Genesis 3: 16, *New Berkeley Version.*

women could not be "one flesh." Yet polygamy—plural wives—was practiced at least as early as the seventh generation by Lamech, a descendant of Cain.[7]

The record mentions only one wife for Noah. Abraham apparently had sex relations with his one wife, Sarah, until barrenness moved her to suggest that he have a child by her handmaiden, Hagar.[8] When Hagar became pregnant she "despised" her mistress, not because of the sexual opportunity with Abraham, but because she was proven fertile. Sarah quickly realized her mistake.

Dedicating Man's Sexuality to God

God again reminded Abraham that through a son by Sarah he would become "a father of many nations."[9] This son and all other male descendants should be circumcised by cutting away the loose skin at the end of the penis eight days after birth. Circumcision, God said, "shall be for a covenant sign between Me and you."[10]

Today circumcision is considered a hygienic measure in modern hospitals and is routinely done on newborn male babies. Abraham and his Hebrew descendants saw it as a religious act. The removal of the foreskin marked a person as a member of the covenant people, and was a token reminder that the reproductive powers of the male belonged to God. The penis was the organ of man's body to be used in fulfilling God's covenant promise. It was considered sacred and inviolate.

Did God Look Away from Sexual Intercourse?

The Hebrews considered sex within marriage to be

[7]Genesis 4: 23.
[8]Genesis 16: 2.
[9]Genesis 17: 5.
[10]Genesis 17: 11, *New Berkeley Version.*

23

natural. "Know,"[11] "lie with,"[12] or "go in unto,"[13] were Hebrew terms for the most intimate relationship between man and woman. The celebrated sex researchers Johnson and Masters are correct in noting, "The Old Testament view of sex did not oppose sexual expression in marriage. . . . The Bible speaks of three obligations a husband must fulfill when he marries: he must provide a wife with food, clothing, and conjugal relations."

Sex in Marriage

The earliest Old Testament marriages involved a simple agreement between the parents of the couple and the exchange of gifts. The marriage of Isaac and Rebekah is a beautiful example. There is no record of vows being spoken, nor of a formal ceremony. Isaac brought Rebekah into his mother's tent where the marriage was consummated in sexual union. The phrase "he loved her" in Genesis 24: 67 speaks volumes.

In later Hebrew history marriage included elaborate ceremonies. The couple was betrothed in a binding covenant months before the wedding. The marriage was not regarded as complete until the couple had their first sexual union. This usually occurred on the first night of the wedding festivities in a special room called the bridechamber.

There were several rules relating to ritual cleanness. After intercourse, a husband and wife must bathe with water.[14] Intercourse was prohibited before, during, and after the menstrual period—about seven days each month.[15] Intercourse was not permitted until 40

[11]Genesis 4: 1.
[12]Leviticus 18: 22.
[13]Genesis 29: 23.
[14]Leviticus 15: 18.
[15]Leviticus 15: 19-24.

24

days after the birth of a boy, and 80 days after the birth of a girl.[16]

Men were required to abstain from sex during certain times of fasting. Intercourse was prohibited for soldiers in battle.[17] Some modern football coaches ask their players to refrain from sexual intercourse for two or three days before a game.

Neither the male nor female sex organs are directly named in the Old Testament. Organs of both sexes are euphemistically referred to as "flesh"[18] and "feet"[19] in several places. The penis is called a "member" in Deuteronomy 23: 1. The testicles are "stones" in the same verse. The penis and testicles are "secrets" ("private parts"—RSV) in Deuteronomy 25:11.

Where Was the Stork?

The Jews believed that more than sexual intercourse was required for conceiving a child. They felt that it took God's direct act to open the woman's womb. A barren woman was always suspected of being out of God's favor.

The greatest event of a husband's life was when he became a father. His status, prestige, and success in life were measured by the number of his children. A large progeny was evidence of God's blessing.

"Lo, children are an heritage of the Lord: and the fruit of the womb is his reward. As arrows are in the hand of a mighty man; so are children of the youth. Happy is the man that hath his quiver full of them: they shall not be ashamed, but they shall speak with the enemies in the gate. . . . Thy wife shall be as a

[16]Leviticus 12.
[17]II Samuel 11: 11.
[18]Leviticus 15: 2, 19.
[19]Deut. 28: 57; Judges 3: 24; I Samuel 24: 3; Isaiah 7: 20.

fruitful vine by the sides of thine house: thy children like olive plants round about thy table."[20]

Consequently, a barren Hebrew woman felt bitter disappointment when she could not conceive a child. The classic example is Hannah, one of Elkanah's two wives. Elkanah "loved" barren Hannah. Year after year Hannah went up to the house of the Lord to pray, weep, and fast in hopes that God would give her a child. Finally, she vowed that if God would "remember" her and give her a son, she would dedicate him to special service. After Eli the priest told her the prayer was heard, she went home and conceived a son, "Because I have asked him of the Lord,"[21] who became the first great prophet of Israel since Moses.

It was not unusual for a man to have more than one wife as Elkanah did. A man did not necessarily take a second wife because his first wife was barren. In some cases, such as Abraham and Sarah, the husband had sexual intercourse with a servant girl in hopes of producing posterity. Abraham's grandson Jacob had children by handmaidens of both of his wives, Leah and Rachel. Rachel envied Leah for having borne Jacob children and offered her maid Bilhah, "that I may also have children by her."[22] Later, Leah stopped bearing and gave her maid Zilpah to Jacob in hopes of increasing her progeny. Sisterly rivalry was involved here. When Rachel finally did conceive and give birth, she rejoiced and said, "God hath taken away my reproach."[23]

Fatherhood by Proxy

The Jews felt that every husband was entitled to progeny, even if he did not produce children during his lifetime. The dead man's brother or nearest male

[20]Psalm 127: 3-5; 128: 3.
[21]I Samuel 1: 20.
[22]Genesis 30: 3.
[23]Genesis 30: 23.

kin was required to marry his widow and raise up seed in his name. This was called a levirate marriage. A brother who refused to perform this duty was summoned before the elders. If he declared, "It is not my desire to take her," then the widow was allowed to loosen his sandal, spit in his face, and say, "So shall it be done to the man who refuses to build up his brother's house." After that his name was to be known in Israel as "the family of the unshod."[24]

One of the best-known Old Testament love stories concerns a levirate marriage. Ruth, a young widow, elected to become a servant of her dead husband's family. Boaz, a wealthy kinsman of her husband, fell in love with her and gave her special privileges in gathering grain in his fields.

Ruth's mother-in-law Naomi wanted her to marry the rich landowner, but another kinsman stood closer in line. She advised Ruth to get prettied up and slip down to the threshing floor where Boaz was sleeping and lie at his feet. When Boaz discovered Ruth, he was pleased. He asked her to remain until morning when he promised to ask that the kinsman ahead of him make a decision about Ruth's future.

The near kinsman relinquished his right to marry Ruth to Boaz. Boaz and Ruth were married and from their line came Jesus of Nazareth.

Desperate Widow

The tragic events following the death of Er, Judah's eldest son, stand in sharp contrast to the beautiful love story of Ruth and Boaz.

After the wicked Er's death by divine punishment, his father asked Onan, his brother, to marry the widow Tamar "and raise up seed to thy brother."[25] Onan knew that the child conceived would not be

[24]Deuteronomy 25: 5-10, *New Berkeley Version.*
[25]Genesis 38: 8.

considered his, but his dead brother's. He stopped short in the midst of intercourse and "spilled it [his semen] on the ground, lest that he should give seed to his brother."[26]

This interruption was considered insulting to the widow Tamar, disloyal to his dead brother, and disobedient to God. Scripture says that what he did displeased God and God took his life.

Some interpreters have incorrectly deduced that Onan died because he practiced a form of birth control. Some have suggested that his sin was masturbation. The context, plus an understanding of the levirate law, shows his sin was a refusal to provide his dead brother a descendant.

The story does not end with the death of Er. Judah, now a widower, had a third and younger son, Shelah. He was reluctant to send the boy to the desperate widow. Furious at her father-in-law, Tamar threw off her widow's garments and disguised herself as a harlot. She accosted Judah by the roadside and enticed him to give her a pledge of payment for sexual privilege. Later, after the widow was discovered to be pregnant, Judah learned that she had played the harlot. In angry self-righteousness he exercised his authority as head of the clan and ordered her to be burned. Tamar then declared that Judah was the father of her unborn child and displayed his pledge as proof. Judah, chagrined, admitted his mistake in not giving his younger son to her.

A Double Standard?

Consorting with a harlot was not then considered a terrible sin for a man, but the double standard never had divine approval.

The woman's role in reproduction was seen as subsidiary to the man who planted his seed. She merely

[26]Genesis 38: 9.

28

carried *his* child. This, instead of inferior intelligence, is probably the main reason why women were considered to be less important than men in the Biblical world of the Middle East.

In adultery a man sinned against God and his paramour's husband. The adulterer's unfaithfulness to his wife was not an issue. The Seventh Commandment, "Thou shalt not commit adultery,"[27] can only be understood in the light of the Tenth Commandment, "Thou shalt not covet thy neighbour's wife."[28] The wife was the husband's most precious possession. He and he alone had the right to her God-given powers of reproduction. It was a terrible crime for another man to introduce alien seed into his lineage. Not even the king had the right to violate an ordinary citizen's lineage. Thus David sinned not against the royal wives but against Uriah when he lay with Bathsheba.

The husband could plant his seed in a female possession of lesser value—his wife's handmaid, a concubine, or a slave—though the children of his legitimate wife (or wives) would hold higher inheritance rights.

Wisdom in Old Age

The ordinary Hebrew could not support numerous wives and concubines. Kings could, but they were warned by God not to "multiply wives" lest the "heart be turned away."[29] Despite the warning, many Hebrew kings, notably Solomon, followed the culture of the Middle East and filled their palaces with wives and concubines. Solomon loved "many strange [foreign] women"[30] and accumulated 700 wives and princesses and 300 concubines who "turned away his heart after other gods."[31]

[27]Exodus 20: 14.
[28]Exodus 20: 17.
[29]Deuteronomy 17: 17, *New Berkeley Version.*
[30]I Kings 11: 1.
[31]I Kings 11: 3, 4.

There is an old poem by James Ball Naylor that aptly describes the misadventures of David and Solomon.

King David and King Solomon led merry,
  merry lives,
With their many, many lady friends,
And their many, many wives;
But when old age crept up on them
With its many, many qualms,
King Solomon wrote the Proverbs;
  and King David wrote the Psalms.

In his old age King Solomon realized his mistakes and in his Proverbs proclaimed the virtues of fidelity in marriage and warned against the allurements of strange women. For example:

"The lips of a strange woman drop as an honeycomb, and her mouth is smoother than oil: But her end is bitter as wormwood, sharp as a two-edged sword. Her feet go down to death; her steps take hold on hell. . . . Drink waters out of thine own cistern, and running waters out of thine own well [euphemisms for sexual intercourse]. . . . Let thy fountain be blessed: and rejoice with the wife of thy youth. Let her be as the loving hind and pleasant roe; let her breasts satisfy thee at all times; and be thou ravished always with her love."[22]

A Woman's Jewel

Naturally a Hebrew man expected his bride to be a virgin. It was her father's responsibility to bring her to marriage unviolated by any man. A woman's chastity was her most precious possession. Without virtue, she ranked very low in the marriage market.

There is no direct account in the Old Testament of a ritual that established a bride's virginity. However, it seems that a traditional method did exist. Deuteron-

[22]Proverbs 5: 3-5, 15, 18, 19.

omy 22: 13-21 projects a possible legal situation where a bridegroom charges that he did not find in his bride "evidences of virginity."[23] The onus was put upon the girl's parents to produce the "proofs of her virginity and lay them before the elders at the gate of the city."[24]

Apparently bloodstained garments, "proof" of virginity, were given to the bride's parents after the couple's first sexual union. The parents kept them in case the bridegroom should later seek an excuse to be rid of his wife.

Today in parts of the Middle East it is still the custom for the bride's mother to hurry in the morning to the bridal bed and gather up the bloodstained *sharshef* for proof of her daughter's virginity. The blood would come from the piercing of the hymen membrane which covers part of the vagina of most, but not all, chaste young women.

Stern Punishment

The Mosaic code required that a bride proven unchaste be stoned to death by the men of her city for committing "a flagrant crime in Israel, playing the harlot in her own home."[25]

In the case of a man caught "lying" with a married woman, both were put to death. If a man had intercourse with a betrothed virgin in a city where she could call for help but did not, both were put to death. If a man raped a betrothed woman and she called in vain for help, only he should die. If the woman was a virgin and not betrothed, the man was required to pay the girl's father 50 shekels of silver, and take her as his wife.[26]

[23]Deuteronomy 22: 14, *New Berkeley Version.*
[24]Vs. 15, *Ibid.*
[25]Deuteronomy 22: 21, *New Berkeley Version.*
[26]Deuteronomy 22: 22-29.

A Symbol of Spiritual Adultery

Generally, adultery in the Old Testament is shown as a violation against another man's property. Here and there are found evidences of a higher view. Joseph, when confronted by the frank invitation of his Egyptian master's wife to "Lie with me," refused by saying, "How . . . can I do this great wickedness, and sin against God?"[37] When she persisted, he ran out of the house.

During the time of Jeremiah the chosen people lapsed into promiscuous living. Men "trooped to the houses of harlots. They were well-fed lusty stallions, each neighing for his neighbor's wife. Shall I not punish them for these things? says the Lord; and shall I not avenge myself on a nation such as this?"[38]

The prophets saw the union of man and wife as symbolic of Israel's relationship with God. They declared that the marital unfaithfulness so prevalent in the declining years of the nation were symbolic of Israel's spiritual adultery in turning to idols.

Two Kinds of Harlots

Harlotry and prostitution were common in the Middle East of Old Testament days. Yet there were few harlots among the Israelites. Girls were expected to marry soon after attaining puberty. Consequently, there were few unattached women in Hebrew society.

A man was not ostracized or condemned by his peers for having sex with a common harlot. The Hebrew spies were hidden by a harlot. During the evil times of later Hebrew history harlotry became more prevalent. However, there is no indication that God condoned harlotry. To the contrary, He pronounced judgment upon both men and their prostitutes.

Involvement of a Hebrew man with a fertility-cult

[37]Genesis 39: 7-9.
[38]Jeremiah 5: 7-9, RSV.

prostitute was abhorred even more than a liaison with an ordinary harlot. The tribes around Israel in Canaan practiced religious prostitution. The pagans saw a relationship between the seed of corn planted in the ground and the male seed planted in a woman's body. They thought that intercourse between a woman dedicated to the agriculture deities might move the gods to bless them with good crops.

A Hebrew man bore on his circumcised penis the mark of God's covenant with Israel. To use that dedicated organ in a sexual ceremony that implored the favor of a pagan god was apostasy of the worst sort. Thus when God thundered His judgment against Hebrews who went "awhoring," He also had in mind religious purity.

Sordid Sex Sins

Under the Mosaic law sexual relations with a close relative was punishable by death. Incest included sexual relations with a man's step-mother, half sister, and daughter-in-law, or with a blood relative.[39]

Homosexuality was also an "abomination" and punishable by death. "If a man lies with a male as with a woman, both of them have committed an abomination; they shall be put to death."[40] Some cities of Biblical times were infamous for rampant homosexuality —Sodom and Gibeah for example.[41]

Lesbianism (female homosexuality) is not mentioned in the Old Testament. It may not have been a problem. Certainly homosexuality among both sexes was less likely to be frequent in a society where male and female identities were strongly established.

Interestingly, the Mosaic law prohibited wearing the clothing of the opposite sex. "A woman shall not wear men's clothing nor shall a man put on a woman's

[39]Leviticus 20: 11-21.
[40]Leviticus 20: 13, RSV.
[41]Genesis 19: 4-8; Judges 19: 16-26.

dress; for anyone doing such things is abhorrent to the Lord your God."[42] The age of unisex had not arrived!

The Hittite law, which antedates the Mosaic code by many years, prescribed the death penalty for sexual intercourse with an animal, but permitted the king to pardon the offender. There was no pardon for the Hebrew man or woman caught performing this sordid sex perversion. "Whoever lies with a beast shall be put to death."[43]

Homosexuality and bestiality were extensively practiced by the Canaanite nations. "Do not defile yourselves by any of these things," God warned Israel, "for by all these the nations I am casting out before you defiled themselves; and the land became defiled, so that I punished its iniquity, and the land vomited out its inhabitants. . . . So keep my charge never to practice any of these abominable customs . . . and never to defile yourselves by them: I am the Lord your God."[44]

Sex Can Be Beautiful

The Old Testament also presents the beautiful side of sex as it is experienced in marriage.

The sexiest book in the Bible is the Song of Solomon. Some theologians have been embarrassed at the frank language and have sought to find reasons for excluding it from the Biblical canon. Others have gotten off the sexual "hook" by calling the book a mystical allegory of God's love for Israel, Christ's love for His Church, or Christ's love for the believer. The most obvious explanation is that the book portrays love as God plans it for husband and wife.

The Song is a collection of love poems in which the lovers live in constant wonder at belonging to each

[42]Deuteronomy 22: 5, *New Berkeley Version.*
[43]Exodus 22: 19, *RSV.* (See also Leviticus 18: 23; 20: 15, 16.)
[44]Leviticus 18: 24, 25, 30, *RSV.*

other. Many of the lines express a bride's thoughts on love as she delights in sexual relations with her beloved.

The husband and wife of this Song desire one another exclusively. Each sees the other as a sensuous, exciting person who can compare with no one else.

The husband sings to his beloved:

How much more delicious is your love than
    wine;
And the fragrance of your ointments than all
    the rich spices.
Your lips drop honey, my bride,
Honey and milk are under your tongue.[45]

She responds,

My lover is fair and ruddy,
The choicest among ten thousand.
His head is finest gold,
His locks are wavy, black as a raven.
His eyes are like doves beside brooks of
    water,
Washed with milk and fitly set.
His cheeks are like a bed of spices,
Like banks of sweetest herbs;
His lips are lilies dropping liquid myrrh.
His hands are rods of gold, set with gilded
    stones,
His body is as polished ivory, overlaid with
    sapphires.
His limbs are pillars of marble, set in sockets
    of gold.
His stature is like Lebanon, as striking as
    the cedars.
His mouth is all sweetness, and he is most
    lovely.[46]

Within the intimacy of marriage the naked body bears no shame. The husband exults,

[45]Song of Solomon 4: 10, 11, *New Berkeley Version.*
[46]Song of Solomon 5: 10-16, *New Berkeley Version.*

35

O maiden of queenly form!
Your rounded thighs are a jeweled chain,
The work of a master craftsman.
Your navel is as a rounded bowl,
In which mingled wine is never lacking;
Your belly as a heap of wheat, set about with
    lilies.
Your breasts are as two fawns, the twins of
    a gazelle;
Your neck is as a tower of ivory.[47]
She calls back,
I belong to my beloved, and his desire is for
    me.
Come, my beloved, let us go out into the fields,
Let us lodge among the hennas. . . .
There will I give you my love.
The mandrakes [love apples] give forth their
    fragrance;
At our doors are all kinds of choice fruits,
Fresh and ripe they are, too, my beloved;
All of these I have laid up for you.[48]

The love of these poems is not casual sex, not the mere gratification of physical passion. It is deep and serious, lasting and real. The bride warns her girl friends twice of the foolishness of awakening or stirring up love, "until love itself shall please."[49] She wants them to wait until love is in full bloom and can be enjoyed in the delightful commitment of marriage.

The bad and the beautiful, the sweet and the sordid—the Old Testament tells about sex as it was actually experienced in Hebrew society. The message is that sex is given by God for procreation and the means for expressing the deepest love within marriage. Perversion of God's gift of sex brings suffering and judgment.

[47]Song of Solomon 7: 1-4, *Ibid.*
[48]Song of Solomon 7: 10-13, *New Berkeley Version.*
[49]Song of Solomon 2: 7; 3: 5, *Ibid.*

CHAPTER THREE

New Testament: What It Says About Sex

The New Testament says much less about sex than the Old. Jesus and His first followers grew up in Jewish homes, communities, and culture. They generally accepted and followed the customs and laws relating to sex and reproduction given in the Jewish Scriptures.

Mary a Perpetual Virgin?

There is no reason to believe that Mary and Joseph abstained from sexual intercourse after Mary's 40-day purification period ended following the birth of Jesus. Their culture saw sex within marriage as a God-given function, and pleasure and procreation as the continuation of God's work. The "one-flesh" concept of marriage continued to be taught by the rabbis. Only one tiny Jewish sect, the Essenes, renounced marriage in the name of holiness. The Essenes did not influence Jesus or the writers of the New Testament to any marked extent, although they probably influenced later Christian attitudes toward sex.

The "Playboy" Romans

Perverted sexual ideas circulated in the world that surrounded the subjugated Hebrews. Roman men practiced the double standard and saw concubines and prostitutes as mere objects for the gratification of male sexual desire. Drunken orgies frequently occurred in upper-class Roman society. Naturally, the same men expected their wives to be virgins and to have sex only in marriage. Excavations in the ruins of Roman cities have revealed pornographic drawings that could not be shown to the public until recent times. Cicero, the philosopher-statesman of the century before Christ, declared in his speech *Pro-Calleo*, "If there is anyone who thinks that young men should be completely forbidden the love of courtesans, he is indeed extremely severe."

Sex Among the Greeks

Greek ideas ranged from one extreme to the other. Strict ascetics said intercourse was never permissible. The Stoics, whom Paul encountered at Athens, conceded that intercourse in marriage alone is permissible and then only for procreation. Dualists who saw the body and soul as separate entities approved of intercourse as long as procreation was avoided. A branch of antinomians (anti-law) preached complete sex freedom. Intercourse in any way for anyone at any time and at any place was desirable. Another branch of antinomians said sexual intercourse in all possible ways was necessary for salvation.

There were numerous nature cults in the first-century world that practiced free sex. The Greek word *porneia*, translated "fornication" in the New Testament and from which comes our word pornography, was used in connection with these cults.

Was Jesus Married?

A new book claims that Jesus was married during some of the "unknown" years between 12 and 30. This is only an unfounded conjecture and nothing more. Another view is that He was an ascetic and with His cousin John the Baptist belonged to the Essenes. If this be true, why did He attend the wedding feast at Cana and use marriage ceremonies as analogies for spiritual truth? Why did He eat and drink with sinners not known for their ascetic ways?

The reason Jesus didn't get married is not that He had no sexual interests, nor was it that He did not enjoy the companionship of a woman. The most logical reasons are that He knew He could not support a wife in the work He had come to do and that He would die at an early age.

Did Jesus have sexual desire? Yes. He "was in all points tempted like as we are."[1] One of the temptations in the wilderness related to physical needs. Sex is one of the greatest hungers of life for any normal man or woman. How else can incarnation—God in human flesh—be explained than to say that Jesus was a real man with manly desires?

Christians still suffering from Victorian prudery may find it shocking to think that Jesus had sex organs. Certainly He did. Certainly the humanity in Jesus must have desired fulfillment of natural urges. Certainly He was tempted to indulge in both imaginary and real sex, but what makes Jesus different from the rest of mankind is that He never misused His sexuality or did anything contrary to God's will for Him. The deity in Jesus maintained control.

What a comfort for any red-blooded young man or woman to know that "because he himself has suffered and been tempted, he is able to help those who are tempted."[2]

What Did Jesus Say About Sex?

Jesus didn't avoid the subject of sex, nor did He dwell on it. What He said is extremely significant.

Jesus never revoked the Old Testament commandments on sex. "Think not that I am come to destroy the law, or the prophets: I am not come to destroy, but to fulfil."[3]

Specifically, Jesus never made an exception of the Seventh Commandment. He quoted it,[4] placed adul-

[1]Hebrews 4: 15.
[2]Hebrews 2: 18, RSV.
[3]Matthew 5: 17.
[4]Matthew 19: 18.

39

tery within the context of defiling sins,[5] and extended it to the thought life of man.

"You have learned that they [our forefathers] were told, 'Do not commit adultery.' But what I tell you is this: If a man looks on a woman with a lustful eye, he has already committed adultery with her in his heart. If your right eye is your undoing, tear it out and fling it away; it is better for you to lose one part of your body than for the whole of it to be thrown into hell. And if your right hand is your undoing, cut it off and fling it away; it is better for you to lose one part of your body than for the whole of it to go to hell."[6]

Jesus traced adultery to its place of origin—the human heart which symbolized the seat of the intellect, the affections, the will. The man who lusts after a woman—imagining how it would be to have intercourse with her and lingering on such thoughts—is guilty. Any person knows that it is possible to imagine an experience until it becomes almost real.

The Rabbis said, "The eye and the heart are two brokers of sin." Add to them the hand (the excitement of touch) and we have three members which play key roles in arousing the sex organs. Better that the eye be torn out and the hand be cut off, Jesus said, if you are going to be led astray by these members. Adultery was sin against God, not just the violation of a neighbor's property.

What Did Jesus Say About Marriage?

"Haven't you read," Jesus reminded the Pharisees who were quizzing him about divorce, "that the one who created them from the beginning made them male and female and said: 'For this cause shall a man leave his father and mother, and shall cleave to his wife; and the twain shall become one flesh'? So they are no longer two separate people but one. No man

[5]Mark 7: 21.
[6]Matthew 5: 27-30, *New English Bible*.

therefore must separate what God has joined together."[7] Jesus affirmed that marriage was to be a lifelong partnership, with love expressed in the union of "one flesh"—sexual intercourse. The relationship was God-ordained and must not be broken by man.

Jesus never said that celibacy was better than marriage. Nor did He consider singles second-rate citizens. Three single adults—the sisters Mary and Martha and their brother Lazarus—were among His best friends. He did say that God and His Kingdom should hold priority above all human relationships.[8]

Did Jesus Permit Divorce?

Before Moses, the Hebrews were very loose on divorce. A man could simply tell his wife to leave. The Mosaic code protected a wife against the mere whim of a disgruntled husband by requiring a divorce certificate that took time for arranging. This interim offered opportunity for reflection and possible retraction. By the time of Christ, the rabbis had made it possible for a man with political or religious clout to get a divorce certificate quickly for the most trivial reasons. He might not like his wife's cooking, for example, or he might find a more attractive woman.

"I say to you," Jesus declared, "that every one who divorces his wife, except on the ground of unchastity, makes her an adulteress; and whoever marries a divorced woman commits adultery."[9] The last phrase may have been aimed at men who arranged for married women they wished to marry to get divorce certificates.

What is left unclear is whether Jesus allowed for remarriage of the innocent party to a single person or someone whose mate had died.

[7]Matthew 19: 4-6, *Phillips.*
[8]Luke 14: 26.
[9]Matthew 5: 32, *RSV.*

41

Did Jesus "Write Off" Sexual Sinners?

Jesus welcomed those who committed sexual sins, just as He did all other sinners. He regarded them more kindly than certain hypocritical religionists who bent God's laws to satisfy their passions while demanding full punishment for transgressors.

Recorded in John's Gospel are two significant encounters of Jesus with sexual sinners. He invited the Samaritan woman at the well to "drink" from the "water" that "will be an inner spring always welling up for eternal life."[10] When Jesus pointed out that she had had five husbands and was then living with a man illicitly, she did not sense that He was condemning her. Her response instead was, "Sir, I perceive that you are a prophet."[11]

The second woman was brought to Him by the scribes and Pharisees after they had caught her having intercourse with a man. Nothing is said about the woman's paramour. Perhaps they let him escape. The accusers had no compassion for the woman. They had a court for the trial of such cases, but it was sometimes customary to ask the opinion of a rabbi. Finding Jesus in the Temple, they saw an opportunity to trap Him.

"Teacher, this woman has been caught in the act of adultery," they said. "Now in the law Moses commanded us to stone such. What do you say about her?"[12]

Jesus knew that stoning was the penalty required under the Mosaic law. Doubtless His enemies felt He would show compassion and ask that she be released. Should He suggest mercy, they could then charge Him with law-breaking.

Jesus stooped down and wrote on the ground. Tra-

[10]John 4: 14, *New English Bible.*
[11]John 4: 19, *RSV.*
[12]John 8: 4, 5, *RSV.*

42

dition says that the woman was a betrothed virgin and that He wrote the names and sins of her accusers on the ground.

They continued asking Him about the fate of the woman until finally He straightened to face them and said, "He that is without sin among you, let him first cast a stone at her."[13]

It was the perfect answer both then and now for those who see sexual sin as unforgivable.

Jesus stooped again to write. When He looked up, only the woman was left. "Woman, where are they?" He asked. "Has no one condemned you?" She said, "No one, Lord." And Jesus said, "Neither do I condemn you; go, and do not sin again."[14]

Will There Be Sex in Heaven?

An answer to this question comes from a discussion between Jesus and the Sadducees who did not believe in life after death. Hoping to trick the Lord, they posed a puzzler on levirate marriage. One of seven brothers died childless. Each of his brothers in turn married the widow and died childless. Finally the woman herself died. The question: "'In the resurrection, therefore, to which of the seven will she be wife? For they all had her." Jesus answered, "You are wrong, because you know neither the scriptures nor the power of God. For in the resurrection they neither marry nor are given in marriage, but are like angels in heaven."[15]

Sex Scandals in the Early Church?

The first church leaders and the members of the Jerusalem congregation devoutly kept the Law and lived pure lives. Problems came when the church moved into the Gentile world where pagan philoso-

[13]John 8: 7.
[14]John 8: 10, 11, RSV.
[15]Matthew 22: 28-30, RSV.

phies prevailed. New Christians had to learn the meaning of personal purity. Some false teachers twisted Scripture to justify loose living.

The greatest problems occurred in the church at Corinth, a commercial city of wealth, luxury, and immorality. No other city rivaled Corinth's reputation in vice. To "live like a Corinthian," meant to live a life of promiscuity and debauchery. Stage plays were little more than drunken orgies. The cast of "Oh, Calcutta!" would have felt right at home.

Poseidon, the god of the sea, was Corinth's honorary deity, but the greatest devotion was given to Aphrodite, the goddess of sensual love.

The Corinthians believed that Aphrodite had risen from the foam of the sea where Uranus' blood had fallen after he had been mutilated by Cronus. More than a thousand priestess prostitutes performed in Aphrodite's temple.

Paul established the church at Corinth on his second missionary journey. After he left, reports came to him about serious problems in the congregation. One man had become sexually involved with his stepmother, "immorality such as even pagans do not tolerate,"[16] Paul said. He asked them to get rid of the violator immediately, for "a little leaven leaveneth the whole lump."[17] In the same chapter he told them not to associate with immoral church members, adding that he did not mean "the immoral of this world . . . since then you would need to go out of the world."[18] In Corinth it was practically impossible not to associate with sexual sinners, but in the midst of impurity, they could keep pure.

Was Paul Cynical About Sex?

Paul has been called a crusty old bachelor with

[16] I Corinthians 5: 1, *New English Bible*.
[17] I Corinthians 5: 6.
[18] I Corinthians 5: 10, RSV.

44

warped ideas on sex. This is hardly fair when you consider the man, his writings, and his belief that Christ would be returning in a short time.

The apostle may have been married as a young man and became a widower before starting his missionary journeys. Evidence comes from his defense before King Agrippa. In recalling his opposition to Christians, he said, "I cast my vote against them."[19] Paul could have been referring to his vote as a member of the Sanhedrin, the high Jewish religious court to which only married men belonged. However, if he had been a member of that august body, it does seem he would have mentioned this in one of the passages describing his life before he met Christ. There is no evidence that his "thorn in the flesh" was a wife. "Three times I besought the Lord . . . that *it* should leave me,"[20] he said. The "thorn" was surely not a person.

Nor had Paul been guilty of sexual indiscretions. Had this been the case, his enemies would have discredited him in every city. "As to righteousness under the law" he declared himself "blameless."[21]

Paul was a Jew by heritage and practice who classified adultery (violation of the marriage bond) and fornification (usually this meant sex among or with the unmarried) with such things as idolatry, murders, and drunkenness.[22] He believed that marriage was for keeps. "For the woman which hath an husband is bound by the law to her husband so long as he liveth."[23]

He realized the need for married couples to enjoy regular sex relations. "The husband must give the wife what is due to her, and the wife equally must give the husband his due. The wife cannot claim her

[19]Acts 26: 10, RSV.
[20]II Corinthians 12: 8, RSV.
[21]Philippians 3: 6, RSV.
[22]Galatians 5: 19-21.
[23]Romans 7: 2.

body as her own; it is her husband's. Equally, the husband cannot claim his body as his own; it is his wife's. Do not deny yourselves to one another, except when you agree upon a temporary abstinence in order to devote yourselves to prayer; afterwards you may come together again; otherwise, for lack of self-control, you may be tempted by Satan."[24]

Those who see Paul as a sex cynic point to this statement: "To the unmarried and the widows I say that it is well for them to remain single as I do. But if they cannot exercise self-control, they should marry. For it is better to marry than to be aflame with passion."[25]

Did he mean that celibacy is a higher spiritual state than marriage? Or that marriage is only a refuge for those who cannot control their sexual desires? Paul also told the Corinthian Christians, "If you, a man, should marry, don't think that you have done anything sinful. And the same applies to a young woman. Yet I do believe that those who take this step are bound to find the married state an extra burden in these critical days, and I should like you to be as unencumbered as possible."[26]

Paul was not against marriage. He even warned Timothy about false teachers who would forbid Christians to marry.[27] And he instructed him that a pastor or deacon should be the husband of one wife.[28] Paul, in fact, had no patience with the super-pious who felt Christians should leave their unbelieving mates for the sake of the Gospel. "If any brother has a wife who is an unbeliever, and she consents to live with him, he should not divorce her." He said the same regarding a Christian wife with an unbelieving husband.[29]

[24]I Corinthians 7: 3-5, *New English Bible*.
[25]I Corinthians 7: 8, 9, *RSV*.
[26]I Corinthians 7: 28, *Phillips*.
[27]I Timothy 4: 3.
[28]I Timothy 3: 2, 12.
[29]I Corinthians 7: 12-15, *RSV*.

46

Remember that Paul was speaking from the viewpoint of a nomadic missionary who constantly pushed himself to evangelize the Gentiles. Furthermore, he believed that judgment would soon come upon wicked cities such as Corinth and that Christ's return was imminent. Marriage didn't seem to be the most important thing in the world to a man with these views. It is unfair to lift Paul's statements from this context and apply them to Christians living in a different world.

Was Paul a Woman Hater?

Paul's views on women must be understood against the background of the times in which he lived. It was a breach of culture and tradition for women to speak in the congregation and to assume dominance over their husbands or any man. Prostitutes were known for their short hair; therefore, Christian women must not copy after them.

Paul's view of sex was so high that he said the implications of the "one-flesh" union applied even when a man had casual sex with a prostitute.[30] His view of the sanctity of marriage was so great that he compared the relationship of husband and wife to Christ and His Church. He called for wives to be subject to their husbands "as the church is subject unto Christ," and for husbands to love their wives, "even as Christ also loved the church, and gave himself for it."[31] The noblest essay ever written on love is contained in the apostle's first letter to the Christians in the vice-ridden city of Corinth.[32]

Keeping Clean in a Cesspool

Casual sex was available to almost anyone in first-century Corinth, Thessalonica, and other Greco-

[30]I Corinthians 6: 16.
[31]Ephesians 5: 24, 25.
[32]I Corinthians 13.

47

Roman cities. Sexual gratification was linked to the religion of the majority. Chastity was not the way to win a popularity contest. Some teachers even said that freedom in Christ permitted free sex. They even used Christ's statement in Matthew 5: 42 (the Gospels were circulated then only by parchment and word of mouth): "Give to the man who asks anything from you" (*Phillips*), in persuading Christian women.

Paul replied, "As a Christian I *may* do anything, but that does not mean that everything is good for me to do. . . . But you cannot say that our physical body was made for sexual promiscuity; it was made for God, and God is the answer to our deepest longings. The God who raised the Lord from the dead will also raise us mortal men by his power. Have you realized the almost incredible fact that your bodies are integral parts of Christ himself? Am I then to take parts of Christ and join them to a prostitute? Never!

". . . Avoid sexual looseness like the plague! . . . Have you forgotten that your body is the temple of the Holy Spirit, who lives in you, and is God's gift to you, and that you are not the owner of your own body? You have been bought, and at what a price! Therefore bring glory to God . . . in your body."[33]

Control Is the Name of the Game

To young converts who had grown up in a society where sexual promiscuity was considered normal, Paul said, "God's plan is to make you holy, and that entails first of all a clean cut with sexual immorality. Every one of you should learn to control his body, keeping it pure and treating it with respect, and never regarding it as an instrument for self-gratification, as do pagans with no knowledge of God. . . . And you must remember that God will punish all who do offend in this matter. . . . The calling of God is not to

[33] I Corinthians 6: 12-15, 18-20, *Phillips*.

impurity but to the most thorough purity, and anyone who makes light of the matter is not making light of a man's ruling but of God's command. It is not for nothing that the Spirit God gives us is called the *Holy Spirit*."[34]

What About Sexual Perversions?

Every imaginable sexual perversion was practiced in the first-century world. Homosexuality and lesbianism were the most common. Both practices were considered unnatural and evil. Paul included homosexuals (called "effeminate" in the *King James*) in the list of those who would not inherit the kingdom of God.[35] Paul also said that sexual perversion could reach the point of no return. "God has given them up to shameful passions. Their women have exchanged natural intercourse for unnatural, and their men in turn, giving up natural relations with women, burn with lust for one another; males behave indecently with males, and are paid in their own persons the fitting wage of such perversion."[36] The implication here is not that sexual perverts cannot be forgiven and accepted by Christ, but that persistence in perversion will ruin their bodies for the high meaning of sex in the divinely ordained relationship of marriage.

The New Testament, then, extends the Old Testament view of sex. The difference is that the New Testament presents sex in the context of a new relationship between man and God. In this relationship, made possible by Christ's giving of Himself, husband and wife may "know" one another in the new life controlled by the indwelling Holy Spirit.

[34] I Thessalonians 4: 3-8, *Phillips.*
[35] I Corinthians 6: 9.
[36] Romans 1: 26, 27, *New English Bible.*

49

CHAPTER FOUR

The Church Speaks on Sexuality

Chrysostom, the greatest of the Greek church fathers, warned a young man who was bent on marrying a beautiful girl:

"The groundwork of this corporeal beauty is nothing else but phlegm and blood and humor and bile. . . . If you consider what is stored up inside those beautiful eyes, and that straight nose, and the mouth and cheeks, you will affirm the well-shaped body to be nothing else than a whited sepulchre. . . ."

Jerome, the translator of the Latin Vulgate, would not permit couples to partake of the Eucharist for several days after engaging in the "bestial act" of intercourse. "He who too ardently loves his own wife is an adulterer," he declared.

Peter Lombard, the Italian theologian who lived 800 years later, taught that the Holy Spirit left the room when a married couple had sex, even when they intended to conceive a child.

Luther succumbed to marriage, yet he said, "It is impossible to pray upon the marriage bed. It is impossible to have spiritual feelings about what you do with your wife in bed."

Such quotations are embarrassing to us today, but we need to admit that the church has had until very recent times one long hang-up on sex. We also need to admit that there is some truth in Freud's view that the denial and suppression of human sexuality by the church is a major cause of emotional illness.

How Did They Miss the Boat?

Considering the wholesome teaching of both Old

and New Testaments, how did church leaders reach such depressing views?

Simply put: They followed Oriental and Greek dualism instead of the Hebrew view that the natural order of things was established by God.

Alexander the Great's conquering armies had opened up new roads of communication between the Orient and the Greco-Roman world. Oriental ideas fused with Greek concepts saw the creator of the world, the Demiurge, as a being less than God. They thought that Christ had never become a real man, only a phantom.

In the battle over ideas, early church leaders won the battle with paganism over key theological doctrines (the person of Christ as both truly divine and truly human, for example), but lost on sex. Hebrew naturalism, which saw man, body and soul, as a unified whole and sex as a gift of God in a spiritual framework, was shoved aside.

Dualism split the world down the middle and saw division everywhere. The physical world was evil. The spirit world was reality and good. The body with its desires belonged in the physical world and was an evil illusion. Spiritual men must renounce the world and the cravings of the body, especially sexual intercourse. The opposite and curious extreme of this teaching argued that since the body didn't matter one could do as he desired.

Distortions of the Fathers

Instead of reasoning from Scripture, the church fathers sought proof texts to support pagan philosophy.

Augustine (354-430) was the most influential theologian since Paul. He suffered from guilt because of his obsession with sex before his conversion. His revulsion against the lust that had enslaved him must have influenced his ideas on sex. Though he was betrothed at conversion, he wrote in his *Confessions,*

"For my soul's freedom, I resolved not to desire, nor to seek, nor to marry a wife."

He never said that sexual intercourse was the original sin of the first couple. He did conclude that the Fall resulted in a corruption that included unmanageable sexual desire. He also developed the doctrine that sexual desire was the means of passing on original sin from parent to child.

Augustine saw the processes of reproduction as sordid. He expressed horror that the sexual and excretory organs were intermingled.

A World Without Sex

Augustine imagined that if Adam and Eve had not sinned, the human race would have reproduced itself by a method like plant pollination. Jerome and other church fathers felt that God had *originally* planned for humans to reproduce in "angelic fashion" (though they never explained what this meant). They reasoned that God had foreseen the Fall and had made man and woman with the reproductive organs "of the animals they would become."

Augustine believed celibacy to be the best state for man. Still he recognized that marriage was essential on two counts: (1) the generations had to continue and (2) some could not gain control of their sexual passions. He quoted Paul that it was better to marry than burn with uncontrollable passion.

Conditional Sex

However, he said, those who did seek marriage as a safety valve for their sexual impulses were still guilty of venial sin. When this was pardoned, they could have sexual intercourse only for procreation. "Continence from all intercourse," he wrote, "is certainly better than marital intercourse itself which takes place for the begetting of children."

Some married couples saw the "error" of their ways

and made solemn vows of continence. They promised to refrain from sex relations for Christ's sake, while continuing to live in the same household. Some betrothed couples made this commitment before their wedding.

Clement of Alexandria advised Christian husbands to use their wives moderately and only for the sake of raising children. Origen (185-254) said, "Intercourse with the wife only for the sake of a posterity." He forbade a husband to have intercourse with his pregnant wife on grounds this would be an act merely for pleasure.

Two church fathers, Lactantius and Chrysostom (345-407), took exception to this view. Lactantius, writing about 400 A.D., said that God made animals to reject their mates when they were pregnant but made the woman to yield to her husband so he would not be driven to lust after other women. Chrysostom allowed that older people could have intercourse after the time for procreation had passed.

There was unanimous agreement that any form of birth control was wrong. Before his conversion to orthodox Christianity, Augustine followed Manichaean teachings which held that Adam fell because he yielded to sexual desire. The Manichaeans practiced *coitus interruptus* (male withdrawal before ejaculation) in a religious rite. After his conversion Augustine thundered against any form of contraception. A man who tried to prevent conception, he called "an adulterer with his own wife." A wife who tried a form of birth control was "the harlot of her husband." Augustine read between the lines of Genesis 38: 1-10 and declared that God killed Onan for spilling his seed on the ground.

Watch Out for Women

With such a low view of marriage, it was inevitable that women be considered inferior, although Paul had written that "in Christ" there is "neither male nor female."[1] Woman was called "a dangerous species" and "an advanced post of hell" because she had engineered the fall of man. Tertullian (160-230), who is best known for saying, "The blood of the martyrs is the seed of the church," wailed about woman:

"You are the devil's gateway: You are the unsealer of that forbidden tree: You are the first deserter of the divine law: You are she who persuaded him whom the devil was not valiant enough to attack. You destroyed so easily God's image, man. On account of your desert—that is, death—even the Son of God had to die."

To the early Christian theologians, motherhood was the only good purpose which a married woman could fulfill. Augustine wrote: "I do not see in what way it could be said that woman was made for a help for man, if the work of childbearing be excluded." The fathers even found a proof text to emphasize what they saw as woman's primary role: I Timothy 2: 15. The King James version translates this verse: "*She* shall be saved in childbearing, if *they* continue in faith and charity and holiness." Some theologians think this teaches that a woman's salvation, or highest fulfillment, comes when her children continue in the right ways. Theologians still argue over the interpretation of this verse.

The monks who took vows of chastity saw an alluring woman as the agent of the devil to bring about their downfall. They would run from the sight of an approaching woman.

They fled to the desert to be closer to God, yet they could not escape from sexual fantasies. Jerome wrote:

"I . . . fancied myself amongst bevies of dancing maidens. My face was pale and my frame chilled with fasting; yet my mind was burning with the cravings of

[1]Galatians 3: 28.

desire, and the fires of lust that flared up from my flesh was as that of a corpse. So helpless, I used to lie at the feet of Christ, watering them with my tears, wiping them with my hair, struggling to subdue my rebellious flesh with seven days' fasting."

Women were generally not allowed to worship in monastery churches. Some monastic codes prescribed a penalty of 100 to 200 stripes to a monk caught speaking alone with a woman.

Double Vision

Renowned marriage scholar David Mace observes that the church's blurred vision of woman caused it to see double. On one hand sexual woman was viewed as a dangerous trap to be avoided. On the other, non-sexual, virgin woman possessed spiritual graces and was worthy of the highest honor. Woman could not be spiritual and sexual; she must be one or the other.

The view of Mary, the mother of Jesus, figured importantly in the elevating of virginity. When Helvidus denied Mary's virginity after the birth of Christ and mentioned Scripture texts speaking of the "brothers" of Jesus, Jerome called him a blasphemer. Jerome claimed that Joseph was the guardian of Mary, instead of her husband. The doctrine of the Virgin began to grow. Mary became Perpetual Virgin, Advocate, Mediatrix, Mother of Grace, and finally was declared to have ascended into Heaven.

Virginity was praised to the utmost. The virgin birth of Christ was viewed in a negative fashion—a proof that sin had defiled the normal processes of birth. Revelation 14: 4 was used as proof that God delighted in celibacy. Some said Jesus chose His disciples because they were virgin, without explaining how Peter came to have a mother-in-law.[2] The death of a spouse was seen as a second chance for God's best—a life of celibacy.

[2]Matthew 8: 14.

The Doctrine of Celibacy

It was inevitable that sacerdotal celibacy be imposed. If marriage was only for those who couldn't control their base nature, then men in God's service desiring to be holy should not take a wife. The Council of Elvira in Spain (305 A.D.) considered sexual questions and decreed that "all concerned with the ministry of the altar . . . must practice abstinence from their wives . . . or forfeit their positions." By the end of the fourth century this rule was almost universally observed and candidates for the priesthood were forbidden to marry. Later the same rule was imposed upon women desiring to devote themselves to the work of the church.

The Age of Aquinas

The next 900 years were a sterile period for Christian teaching on sex. Augustine's views dominated the church until Thomas Aquinas (1225-74) and his so-called "Schoolmen" systemized Catholic doctrine.,

Aquinas agreed with Augustine on contraceptives. By preventing birth a couple destroyed potential life and removed themselves from a state of grace. Aquinas also exalted virginity, celibacy, and continence in marriage.

Aquinas moderated Augustine's harsh teachings on intercourse. The 13th century scholar was apparently not troubled by personal sex problems as Augustine had been. He tried to mesh Christian doctrine with the philosophy of Aristotle instead of Plato as Augustine had done.

Aquinas conceded to Augustine that concupiscence (sexual lust) was a result of original sin, but insisted that this did not make man's natural sexual tendencies evil. Original sin was transmitted by generation, he said, but it did not necessarily follow that sexual desire was involved.

Following Aristotle, Aquinas said that just as right reason proceeds from man, so the order of nature proceeds from God. Sexual union was therefore instituted by God. Unnatural sex acts would injure God, but natural intercourse within marriage would fall within God's plan. Intercourse with a pregnant or even a sterile wife was natural. So was intercourse between the aged. Preventing insemination during intercourse was unnatural.

Between Aquinas and Luther a few bold churchmen spoke positively on sex. Denis the Carthusian (1402-71) in *The Praiseworthy Life of the Married* emphasized that love between husband and wife should be spiritual, natural, social, and even carnal. He reasoned that the pleasure derived from intercourse is good.

By the 16th century, the Catholic Church had moved slightly away from the thinking of Augustine that sex was legitimate only for procreation. But sex was still officially put on a low level.

Sexless Days

Self-proclaimed celibate church leaders (some had secret mistresses and concubines) had woven a web of confusing regulations around the bedrooms of married couples. Some forbade sex during all holy days and seasons. In addition, continence was advised on Thursday in remembrance of Christ's arrest, on Friday in respect to His Crucifixion, on Saturday in honor of the Virgin Mary, on Sunday in regard to Christ's Resurrection, and on Monday in respect for departed souls. On Tuesday and Wednesday marriage partners were to satisfy their "base instincts."

In view of all this it seems strange that the church had made marriage a sacrament—the sharing of God's creative power. David Mace suggests that "the Catholic theologians, taking the low spiritual view they did of married life, were embarrassed that marriage had been ordained by God, blessed by Christ, and used by Paul as a symbol of the union between Christ and the Church. They solved their problem by exalting marriage as an institution while discouraging it as an enterprise." Karl Barth, the Protestant theologian, concluded that the Catholics had developed a theology of the wedding but not of the marriage.

The historic Council of Trent, which began in 1545, debated sex. Eighteen years later at its end, the bachelor theologians changed little of past teaching. They said that sexual desire was "not sin, but an incentive to sin." They comforted the married with the opinion that sex would not be quite so bad if they would "resist manfully." Celibacy remained spiritually superior to the married state.

Where the Reformers Did Not Reform

Martin Luther started out by agreeing with Augustine, then changed his mind (was it when he saw Katherine?). He said marriage was not a sacrament, but a universal institution which involved pagans and Christians alike. The regulation of marriage, he concluded, should be handled by the civil powers.

However, he continued to agree with Aquinas that the Fall had corrupted man's sexual life. He could not bring himself to see sex as spiritual, calling it a "brute-like quality." Thus he thought it "impossible" to pray upon the marriage bed, but did say that God "winks" at marital intercourse.

He recognized the power of the sex drive, both in himself and in the lives of priests and monks who he knew had common-law wives. So at 42 he married Katherine von Bora, a 27-year-old nun. Luther urged other celibates and monks and priests to follow suit and "relieve their burden of guilt." The Reformer believed that it was better to marry than to let sex desires run amuck.

Luther did not downrate celibacy. He simply felt

that few men, including himself, could remain chaste. He even encouraged divorced people to marry again if they couldn't control their sexual impulses.

Luther broke new theological ground when he emphasized that love is essential in marriage. The more legalistic John Calvin, who also married, agreed with him that love is necessary. Calvin, like Luther, saw celibacy as a high spiritual state, but felt that most would find it necessary to marry. Calvin compiled a list of sexual sins, grading them on an ascending scale of guilt.

The Reformers were more realistic and human in their teaching on sex. Yet they remained tied too closely to Augustine and Aquinas to assert a truly positive doctrine of sex.

The Puritans Liked Sex

The Puritans were born from the theological matrix of Calvinism and in general followed Calvin and Luther's views on sex. They fled persecution in England and founded a colony in the new land. They have been incorrectly stereotyped as stern and ascetic, and frowning upon physical pleasure.

They did have a vendetta concerning women's clothing which was said to encourage "hainous breaches of the Seventh Commandment." A 1650 law forbade women to wear short-sleeved dresses, "whereby the nakedness of the arm may be discovered."

Records in one Puritan church show that the parents of any child born less than seven months after marriage had to confess to fornication. In some such cases at Plymouth, the wife was put in stocks to watch the public whipping of her husband.

Some towns punished adultery by death. Others made offenders wear the scarlet letter "A" for life.

The Puritans were "puritanical" about sex only outside of marriage. They did not see sex between husband and wife as wrong or dirty. Sociologist Morton

Hunt notes the case of a Boston husband being disciplined by his church because he tried "to punish himself for his sins" by refusing to have intercourse with his wife. The congregation judged this to be "unchristian and unnatural" and dismissed him from church membership.

Puritan love letters reveal that husbands and wives were not inhibited in expressing their love in intimate relations. Their one fear was that they might forget God and become idolatrous of their mates.

Jonathan Edwards (1703-58), the noted Puritan preacher, and his wife Sarah enjoyed a beautiful love life. George Whitefield, the bachelor evangelist, visited with them and observed, "A sweeter couple have I not seen." The romance of David Brainerd, the sickly young missionary to the Indians, and Jerusha Edwards, daughter of Jonathan, is one of the great love stories of all times. Jerusha nursed him until his death. Just before dying he whispered to her, "We shall spend a happy eternity together." Jerusha died soon afterwards.

New England winter nights were long and cold. Courting young people were permitted to "bundle"— lie in bed fully clothed, separated by "bundling" boards, and talk. Jonathan Edwards charged that "bundling is one of those things that lead and expose to sin."

The Puritans both in England and America generally had a wholesome view of sex. William Tyndale, the first man to translate the New Testament into English, debated for several years with Thomas More on the issue of whether ministers should marry. Tyndale contended that the Bible encourages pastors to marry and enjoy God's gift of sex. Edmund Spenser, the great Puritan love poet, related divine and human love in his poetry. Anticipating his wedding to Elizabeth Boyle, he longed for the "welcome night, thou night so long expected," and he prayed, "Spread thy broad wing over my love and me, that no man may us see." He wrote, "So let us love, dear love, like as we ought, Love is the lesson which the Lord us taught."

The greatest Puritan writer of all, John Milton, celebrated wedded sexual love in his *Paradise Lost*. Milton saw Adam and Eve before the Fall as enjoying the delights of sexual union.

What About Wesley?

The moral climate grew worse in the 18th century in England. Ribald theater, influential writers who urged free love, and open immorality in high places helped lower sexual restraints to the point where the nation was on the verge of anarchy and revolution. Many historians credit the Wesleyan revivals with saving the nation from the fate of France in this era.

However, no positive teaching on sex emerged from the Wesleyan movement. John Wesley had a notoriously unhappy marriage, in which his long absences must have been a factor. The man who preached 42,000 sermons, wrote 233 books, and rode horseback a quarter of a million miles obviously did not have much time for sex.

The Sexual Hypocrites

Hypocritical Victorianism arose as the fires of revival cooled. The Victorians pretended a purity that never existed. The Victorians idolized the woman as "the guardian of virtue" and "the angel in the house." She was not supposed to have an interest in sex or to enjoy sex relations. She must consider intimate union only as an indulgence to the "beast" in her husband. One story from the Victorian era relates to the wedding night when a groom found his bride lying on the bed, unconscious from chloroform. A note beside her advised, "Momma says you are to do what you like."

The Victorian woman was kept from temptation. Books that dealt with sex in any manner were taboo.

Shakespeare was censored. "Womb," and "belly," and other earthy words were removed from Bibles and prayerbooks. "An interesting condition" was used for the word "pregnant." Tables and pianos had "limbs" not legs. The "limbs" of some furniture might be covered to avoid any impression of nudity. Doctors used dummies so a woman patient could point to the location of pain without having to reveal her own body. Sex and the human body were shameful.

There was another side to the Victorian era. Prostitution flourished while wives looked the other way. Some factory owners made concubines of their working girls. Pornography was a booming business.

The Secular Challenge

The Victorian myth of purity was bound to be shattered. By the early 20th century people were reading Sigmund Freud, George Bernard Shaw, Havelock Ellis, and others who said sex was important and that both men and women should enjoy it.

Birth control movements began picking up speed after the National Birth Control League was founded in 1913. Information on planned parenthood had been circulating to the public since 1840. Woman's suffrage and the Protestant emphasis on the worth and dignity of man were major factors.

Both Protestant and Catholic church leaders reacted strongly, though not for the same reasons. The WCTU, YMCA, and YWCA joined such groups as the Evangelical Alliance and the League for the Protection of the Family to fight "immorality." Some said the use of contraceptives advanced prostitution. Some claimed that Protestants would soon be overwhelmed by Catholics with their large families.

The churchmen could not stem the tide. In 1930 the Protestant Episcopal Church conceded that contraceptives might be used in limited circumstances when justified by morally sound reasons. In 1958 this denomination said contraceptives could be used whenever a couple desired. By this time the public was getting worried about mushrooming population. A few years later the British Council of Churches refused to condemn outright either premarital intercourse or adultery. In 1970 the United Presbyterian Church introduced a study document that included:

—A call for open discussion of sexuality in family groups.

—Admission that premarital virginity is in decline.

—Recognition that extramarital sexual activity may not hurt the interests of the marriage concerned, such as when one partner suffers permanent mental or physical incapacity.

—Concession that some courting couples might "responsibly" engage in premarital intercourse.

—Suggestion that nothing be forbidden in marital relations except that which offends the sensibilities of one's partner.

—Seeing no moral barrier to artificial insemination where a donor's sperm is used to fertilize the wife's ovum.

—Asking that the church explore the possibilities of both celibate and non-celibate communal living arrangements.

The document was hotly debated and sensationalized in the press. Church commissioners finally adopted the report by a vote of 485-259 for study and appropriate action. Then by a 356-349 vote, they reaffirmed the church's "adherence to the moral law of God as revealed in the Old and New Testaments, that adultery, prostitution, fornication, and/or the practice of homosexuality is sin," along with "lust in a man's heart."

The debate in this and other church groups today indicates for better or for worse a radical departure from Augustine's views.

The pendulum has swung.

CHAPTER FIVE

Is There a Sexual Revolution?

Two sensational sex information books top the non-fiction best seller list in the *Time* magazine that arrived as I write. Tonight my family can see the movie "Tom Jones" on NBC television. Or my wife and I can drive a few miles and see "Marriage Manual," "Without a Stitch," "Love (Sexually) Thy Neighbor," "Danish Blue" or one of many other "X" rated films. In a current issue of *McCall's* or *Ladies' Home Journal* we can learn "All About Your Pet's Sex Life," "How Doctors Perform Abortions," "Sex Games People Play" and "Tell Me, Doctor, What about Sex after My Operation?" And if we still aren't aware that this is the sexiest generation ever, we can listen to teenage idols moaning about "making love in the bedroom," or visit a youth hangout and read the buttons as they go by: "Revive Fertility Rites," "Candy is Dandy but Sex Won't Rot Your Teeth," "Chaste Makes Waste," "Love Thy Neighbor But Don't Get Caught." On the way home we can stop at the drugstore and buy toothpaste that gives sex appeal.

Whatever else sex is today, it is certainly big business. Sex is used to sell everything from shoes to automobiles. Imagine a paperback without a nude on the cover! Trade book publishers think a novel won't sell unless it has at least one scene where intercourse is described in the explicit raw. Movie makers say a film won't make money unless a pretty girl "takes it all off."

We hear about the nude stage plays, transsexual operations, hippie communes where sex is all for one and one for all, apartment complexes for singles only

64

where an orgy is just down the hall, mate-swapping clubs, coed college dormitories, proposals of experimental marriages by respected counselors, sex clinics and other nifty little items that are supposed to indicate a phallic Utopia is just around the corner.

The Big Question

Is all this talk about a sexual revolution more show than action? Have Madison Avenue and the pornographic profit makers pulled the fig leaf away from our eyes? Have sexual mores really changed?

Without doubt there is now more being said, read, and seen on the subject of sex than since the days of the Caesars. Perhaps the Western nations have even eclipsed ancient Rome in sensuality. We have the electronic gadgets to do it! Russia and China are too puritanical to be included in any comparison.

Sex! Sex! Sex!

Dr. Morris Fishbein, renowned medical writer, recalls that in 1921, 92 of 96 leading Sunday newspapers censored such words as *ovary, uterus, menstruation,* and *virility* in their articles. Now the pendulum has swung and knocked the censors out of their boxes. Because of recent court decisions, almost anything goes. *The Cleveland Plain Dealer* editorializes: "If you have not looked at the contents of magazine racks lately, you are in for an unpleasant shock. . . . The minds that are at work corrupting youth have been conceived in waste and developed in cattle sheds. They are making fortunes out of a mental sickness for which they should be under treatment."

Even a generation ago sexual misdemeanors were hushed up by the press. Today sexual escapades, both imagined and real, are headlined. In past generations there was certainly a lot of fire but not much smoke of publicity. Today it is just the opposite. As a college chaplain put it, "When all's said and done, there's more said than done."

Dr. David Mace, former executive director of the American Association of Marriage Counsellors, says that what we hear and read "are simply implications of the sexual revolution. The sexual revolution is a revolution in thought and in ideas, as all revolutions are."

Kinsey's Shocker

When it comes to surveys, we must start with the notable (or notorious) Dr. Alfred Kinsey's epochal (or shocking) studies. Kinsey first earned fame in the scientific world by studying the life and habits of the gall wasp. He became a whispered household word for his *Sexual Behavior in the Human Male* (1948) and *Sexual Behavior in the Human Female* (1953). There were a few other researchers before his time, but he stung public opinion.

Kinsey's researchers interviewed over 5,000 men and nearly 6,000 women. He concluded that 51 per cent of unmarried college males and 27 per cent of female collegians were sexually experienced. Kinsey noted that premarital intercourse among women had mounted steadily, but premarital petting of all varieties had *skyrocketed.*

Kinsey found 22 per cent of virginal college coeds blaming their chastity on "lack of opportunity." Over a third of the chaste males in Kinsey's survey gave the same opinion.

Have Times Changed?

It has been two decades since Kinsey's bomb was dropped. What now?

Sociologist Vance Packard reports in *The Sexual Wilderness* (1968) on his survey of 2,200 unmarried juniors and seniors at 21 American colleges and universities. The results showed 57 per cent of the boys sexually experienced, 6 per cent more than Kinsey reported. College females showed a much larger increase, 43 per cent as compared to Kinsey's 27 per cent.

Packard found that 53 per cent of the non-virgin girls had already engaged in intercourse with more than one man. More than a third of the non-virgins admitted having had intercourse with "several" or "many" men.

His conclusion: "If there has been any change in the sexual *behavior* of young people in recent years, it has come mainly from females."

Sex Is Getting Cheaper

Kinsey reported that 22 per cent of his college-level males had patronized a prostitute. Packard's survey showed only 4 per cent. There has been an evident increase in sexual activity among social equals.

Packard found that the most significant change among college students relates to attitudes.

About 50 per cent of the students did not think that "ideally" a bride and groom should both have had their first experience in sex together. Less than half, 47 per cent, of the girls, but only 35 per cent of the boys reporting, said fidelity was the "ideal" after marriage.

Is it "reasonable" for a sexually experienced male to expect his bride to be a virgin? Only 36 per cent of the girls and 21 per cent of the boys said yes; 10 per cent of both sexes called the idea a "preposterous anachronism."

Would they be "troubled" about marrying a person sexually experienced with someone else? A double-standard surfaced: 70 per cent of the boys but only 39 per cent of the girls thought they would.

The major change according to Packard and other authorities has to do with the philosophy that sex is all right so long as no one gets hurt. "Where there is no victim, every act is morally right" is the credo of one student group seeking to legalize a wide variety of sexual acts. Social critic John Keats visited several dozen campuses and came away saying, "Nearly all students and most faculty members today believe that sexual intercourse is not subject to moral judgment."

What About High Schoolers?

Dr. Daniel Offer studied a "typical" group of students during four years of high school. He found that 10 per cent of the group had had sexual intercourse by the end of the junior year and that 80 per cent approved of premarital intercourse, *but* only after graduation. The main reason the teens gave for not "going all the way" during high school was fear that the girl would get pregnant. In another study, Dr. Offer followed 1,500 middle-class teens from 1962-70 and concluded, "There is no evidence to suggest that our teenage population is in the midst of a sexual revolution."

We would expect evangelical church youth to have higher standards. Three studies support this view.

Home Missions magazine queried 130 Southern Baptist youth in three southern churches. Only 8 per cent admitted having had sexual intercourse; 90 per cent said sex relations should not occur before marriage to test physical compatibility; but 31 per cent said petting or fondling just short of intercourse was "all right." In contrast, only 34 per cent of youth in a survey conducted by *Look* magazine vetoes sex before marriage.

Not one of the Baptist youths checked "unimportant" as a characterization of recent changes in sexual attitudes among young people. About half of them marked this "revolutionary."

Drs. Roy B. Zuck and Gene A. Getz profiled 3,000 teens in 416 churches of varying evangelical denominations on their behavior during a six-month period.

Little more than 7 per cent said they had engaged in premarital intercourse with about 25 per cent admitting to masturbation. 42 per cent had petted and necked and 47 per cent had kissed on a first date.

A community study of almost all 16-year-old teens in Webster Grove, Missouri (a St. Louis suburb), revealed similar findings. Only 8 per cent thought sexual intercourse was all right between engaged couples; 40 per cent thought engaged couples should pet. The Webster Grove teens were much more concerned (88 per cent) about getting good enough grades to get into college.

Is Adultery Advancing?

Sociologist Morton Hunt in researching his book, *The Affair,* concluded that nine out of ten husbands cheat on their wives sooner or later. Kinsey estimated 70 per cent. Kinsey also found that about 25 per cent of 1,100 married women had engaged at least once in extramarital sex and another 16 per cent had participated in extramarital petting without coitus. Kinsey's study showed that infidelity by both sexes had been increasing during the 1920-50 period.

Meaningful statistics on the present state of infidelity in marriage in the U.S. are understandably hard to come by. About five years ago 154 agencies of the Family Service Association were asked if they had noted any particular trend in infidelity. Two-thirds said it had become more common during the past ten years and many felt it would increase in the future.

Psychologist Albert Ellis reports from 20 years of counseling that he has heard of more instances of wife-swapping in the past 5 years than in the preceding 15. A number of people have asked him about couples willing to "swap" mates.

A husband and wife reporting team for *The San Francisco Chronicle* during a two-month period "met and corresponded with more than 100 couples who, unaware that they were talking to representatives of a newspaper, unashamedly admitted to being wife-swappers." The couple inserted an ad inviting a swap and received 300 replies, about 100 from married couples.

An interesting conclusion was reached by family specialist Gerhard Neubeck in studying nine young married people who acknowledged being sexually involved outside of marriage. What stood out, Neubeck found, was that most of the nine scored low on strength of conscience.

Serial Polygamy

Divorce has become an institution in America. This year one couple will part legally for every four that will troop to the altar—and many weddings will involve the previously divorced. Only once in American history has the divorce rate been as high as it now is and this was during 1945 when so many war marriages went on the rocks.

Divorce records do not account for all the unhappy marriages—more than 50 per cent some counselors say—that hang together for reasons other than love.

An analogy can be found in Guinea, where the length of a marriage in one tribe hangs on one garment—the bride's wedding gown. The marriage lasts until the gown becomes threadbare. A happy bride wears the gown only rarely, but one who wants to be rid of her husband wears it every day.

Millions of American marriages have become virtually "threadbare," being held together only by the threads of children, job, family, church, or pride.

Sex "therapists" Masters and Johnson estimate that at least one-half of all American marriages suffer from some form of sexual inadequacy such as frigidity in women and impotency in men.

Sodom in San Francisco

Homosexuality is older than Sodom, but it has only recently become "respectable" in some quarters. "Gay" clubs, even "gay" churches, have been springing up all over. There is at least one computerized dating service for homos. Police in San Francisco estimate that more than 10 per cent of the city's 790,000 people are homosexual. Says Dr. William Glasser, in his book *Mental Health or Mental Illness*, "Homosexuality in males is one of the most serious problems in our society."

Babies by Proxy

Artificial insemination is the process by which a baby is conceived apart from normal sexual intercourse. There is little controversy over husband insemination where semen is taken from a husband, who has sperm but cannot fertilize his wife in the usual way, and inserted into the wife's uterus. But artificial insemination by donor (AID) is only recently becoming accepted, with but three states having laws protecting the rights of children produced by this method. An estimated 200,000 AID children are now living with about 20,000 new AID progeny arriving each year. One "fertility specialist" in Pittsburgh says he docs eight to ten inseminations each day from a "bank" in which "donor" sperm, given through masturbation, can be kept alive over two years. At least four other human "sperm banks" are presently in operation with doctors using the same freezing techniques that have been developed for animal semen.

Some scientists see revolutionary new birth processes around the corner. Babies may be "hatched" outside the womb in mechanical "incubators," or borne by "host mothers." In either case the fetus would be removed from the biological parent shortly after conception and transferred to the machine or

71

human "incubator." A movie star could conceive a baby and still preserve her figure.

These, then, are indications that we are in some kind of sexual revolution. Nobel Prize-winner Pearl S. Buck declared in a recent magazine article that no people, with the possible exception of mainland Chinese under Communist rule, have changed so much in the last 20 years as Americans. "Nowhere," she added, "is the change more apparent than in our ethics of sex. The change is so abrupt and far-reaching that we are all dazed by it."

How Did It Happen?

The old Russian peasant log house has a key log running under the center of the floor and sticking out the end. To pull the house down, a tractor jerks this log back and forth until the structure collapses. The word used for shaking the key log is also the word for agitation, meaning "to shake to pieces from underneath."

The structure of sexual controls and traditional mores in America has been shaken by a variety of forces pulling at several key logs.

The Influence of Religion Has Declined

One key log that has been shaken is the power and influence of organized religion. Gallup polls have shown that during a recent ten-year period the number of persons seeing a declining influence of religion rose from 14 to 57 percent.

Related to this factor has been the decline of faith in the authority of Scripture. Before "modern theology" swept into historic Protestant denominations and Judaism, nonbelievers generally respected the Seventh Commandment. Today, many church leaders find exceptions to Scriptural rules and talk broadly of applying humanistic principles to human sexuality. Catholicism has been rocked by a decline of faith in both the authority of church and Scripture. Revolutionary changes of ritual rules, and revocation of time-honored saints such as St. Christopher have moved many Catholics to believe that the Church may be wrong in rules on sex too. The outright challenge of authority by many priests, nuns, and bishops has also shaken the confidence of laymen in their hierarchy.

Home Is No Longer Central

Another key log is home controls. Before the turn of the century most Americans were home-centered farmers and tradesmen. Often the young received their vocational training under parental tutelage. Children were expected to grow up as rapidly as possible and assume responsibilities. School terms were regulated to fit crop cycles. Even the church, which then served as the community social center, was an extension of the home, not its competitor.

Home and family have now lost their historic centrality. The young are quickly fed into the larger society—with school, organized sports, Cub and Brownie Scouts, church clubs, and a host of other groups shaping their minds. The home too often has become the motel where the children eat and sleep. Parents, also occupied with a host of outside activities, have less time to teach by word and example.

Collapse of Community Units

Related to decline of parental and home influence is the breakdown of community units. At one time it was traditional to live one's entire life in a rural community, small town, or urban ethnic neighborhood. The fact that everyone knew everyone was itself a strong control over sexual behavior. No more. Youth leave early for higher education or for job markets in impersonal cities. Family, neighbors, and community influences are left behind.

Rebellion Against the Establishment

More recently youth have been caught up in an anti-establishment mood. The key "log" of authority in general has been shaken by protests and defiance of laws and traditions. Sexual laws, customs, and controls of a past day are winked at and often flaunted under the excuse of individual freedom.

Women Are Moving Up

The status of women has changed tremendously since Victorian days. Women today vote, head households, hold responsible jobs (more than one-third of the labor force), circulate in the business world, and demand equal rights in every way.

Whereas sex was once considered a man's prerogative, now it is also considered a woman's privilege. No longer satisfied to be a man's passive object, women today are more aware of their sexual needs and their potential for sexual enjoyment.

The "Log Shakers"

Exploding knowledge, frank literature, medical advances, revolutionary technology, new movements, and drugs are the "tractors" that have been shaking the structure of traditional sexual morality.

Sigmund Freud (1856-1939) was the most influential of the new thinkers on sex. The Austrian physician saw sex not as restricted to physical feelings, but as a powerful drive profoundly affecting the entire personality.

Havelock Ellis (1859-1939), an English psychologist, studied and wrote about every area of human sexuality, turning up questions that had never been openly asked before.

Kinsey (1894-1956) researched the actual sexual behavior patterns of average people.

New books appeared to challenge the old traditions. Sweden's Elley Key first proclaimed the doctrine of "free love" in her *Love and Marriage,* published in 1911. She called for the individual "to realize his love according to the needs of his *personal* morality." August Bebel, a German socialist, reasoned that "satisfaction of the sexual impulse is everyone's private affair just like the satisfaction of any other natural impulse." Friedrich Engels, the noted Marxist, charged that traditional marriage forced women to be exploited by men.

Bertrand Russell called for the cleansing of sex "from the filth with which it has been covered by Christian moralists." George Bernard Shaw blamed Paul for starting the evils in the marriage system. D. H. Lawrence tried to present sex as an erotic, spiritual experience.

These are some of the major writers who have vastly influenced changes in our sex mores.

Along with new knowledge and literature has come a new direction in education. Exploration and discovery take precedence over rote learning. Youth are told to find out for themselves.

Sex education is already standard curriculum in many schools. Whether good or bad, it is a fact that children are learning more about sexual organs and functions than any young generation in history.

The Sexual Scientists

Medical research has developed new methods of birth control, so that there are now five types available. (1) "Natural" (rhythm) is the only type acceptable to the Catholic church. (2) Mechanical—devices that keep the sperm from reaching the egg. (3) Chemical—solutions that kill sperm. (4) Physiological—oral contraceptives ("the pill") that stop eggs from moving into position for conception. (5) Surgical—abortion, and sterilization of both male and female and vasectomy of the male.

It was never so easy to have sex without reproduction. Just around the corner may be "pills" for the morning after, one for a month or even longer, and "pills" for men.

Antibiotics now are used to treat venereal disease, though they are not as effective as people think they are.

Research has shown that the husband can function sexually into his nineties as long as his wife is interested and interesting.

Most recently, Dr. William Masters and Mrs. Virginia Johnson have observed and written about the sexual functions of couples who have come to their St. Louis clinic for therapy. Masters and Johnson have documented problems never widely discussed before —premature ejaculation, for example, in which the man's orgasm or climax occurs before the woman can fully respond.

Masters and Johnson are the best known "sex therapists." Others are offering services. Sex therapy may soon become so acceptable that practitioners can advertise in the "yellow pages."

Henry Ford Helped

Dr. Abraham Stone used to say that traditional sexual morality was guarded by three fears—fear of conception, infection, and detection. Medical advance has reduced the first two fears in the public mind. Modern technology has helped to reduce the third.

Did Henry Ford ever imagine the part his automobile would play in changing sexual mores? A couple today can be miles away from home in minutes and parked along a secluded lane, whereas their grandparents had to court on the living room sofa, with all the family at home.

If the auto isn't desirable, there's the motel just down the highway. What clerk looks for wedding rings any more?

Technology has also afforded increased leisure time and affluence. Young adults have the time and money to jet to swinging resorts where sex comes easier than in the home community.

The communications revolution produced by technology has probably been the greatest single influence. Entertainment can be viewed in the living room that most people couldn't or wouldn't go see 30 years ago. Drive-ins show X-rated films so boldy that neighbors complain they are tired of seeing sexual intercourse in full color through their back windows. Sex-oriented slick magazines and paperback books can be produced cheaply for the mass market. Advertisers use sex to sell the ever-increasing products of modern technology through both print and broadcast media. There is, for example, the seductive, sultry Swedish girl who begs male viewers to "take it off, take it all off." The product is shaving cream, but the attention-getter is sex.

The "New Morality," Playboy, and Women's Lib

The term "new morality" was actually first used by the Catholic Church in a 1956 decree condemning the relativism in situation ethics, but Bishop John A. T. Robinson popularized the movement in his controversial *Honest to God,* published in 1963. The Bishop of Woolwich suggested that Christian ethics could be boiled down to one principle: responsible love.

Joseph Fletcher published his *Situation Ethics* in 1966 and built on Robinson's ideology. Fletcher, who applied the "new" ethics to many forms of human behavior, foresaw *some* circumstances for *some* people at *some* times when premarital, extramarital, or postmarital sexual relations might not only be acceptable but even desirable. The morality of any form of sex, according to Fletcher, "depends on whether love is fully served."

Baptist theologian Harvey Cox coined the phrase,

"Playboy philosophy." He referred to what he thought was the philosophy of Hugh Hefner and associates who have built a publishing and hotel empire on "entertainment for men." *Playboy* reported gross revenues of $127 million and net profits of $8.5 million for 1970.

Playboy magazine's public affairs director, Anson Mount, says the title "playboy" refers to "that time in life when a young man is out of college. He isn't married yet, or perhaps he's newly married. He hasn't taken on the full responsibilities of adulthood. . . . He has some disposable income, and he's enjoying life.

"We believe," continues Mount, "that sex is by far best in the context of a loving and lasting relationship, but casual sex is not nearly as dangerous as the sexual conservatives would have us think.

"We believe that people are basically good. . . . that human pleasure is good. . . . We don't buy the idea that sexuality is a beast held down within us that we must keep under and must not let out. The traditional legalistic approach to sex is inhuman very often. . . . It's not the fact that a preacher stood in front of you that makes sex moral. It's the quality of the relationship."

Playboy is the leading commercializer of sex and tells an estimated 18 million readers each month that extramarital sex can be fun. Basically, *Playboy* teaches self-gratification for men on the basis that pleasure is the greatest good in life.

Cosmopolitan magazine, edited by *Sex and the Single Girl* author Helen Gurley Brown, fosters the "playgirl philosophy," which essentially follows the theme of *Playboy*.

Women's Liberation is a third and more recent movement that is affecting traditional sexual mores. Lib leader Gloria Steinem says *Playboy* is partly responsible for Women's Lib. "There are times," she adds, "when a woman reading *Playboy* feels a little like a Jew reading a Nazi manual. . . . It's like being on a meat hook."

Lib militants have picketed the Playboy mansion where Hefner and the celebrated bunnies live in Chicago. This doesn't mean that Lib is for traditional sex morals.

Women's Lib asks that women have the same privileges in sex that men have traditionally been accorded—the freedom to initiate sex, to walk out on a man who doesn't satisfy sexually, and in general to decide what is moral and immoral for the individual woman. Some Lib militants have publicly proclaimed themselves to be Lesbians.

Rise of the Drug Culture

The increased use of drugs (alcohol, marijuana, heroin) by both youth and adults has been a factor in changing sex mores. Drug use weakens inhibitions. Addicts turn to prostitution to support their habits. Of course, not all drug users are promiscuous, but they are more likely to be than nonusers.

Now let us consider the "fallout" from the sexplosion that has hit our culture:

More than one and a half million young Americans got into serious trouble in 1970 because they were ignorant of, or would not face the fact that sexual intercourse produces babies. In this age of sexual enlightenment, illegitimate births are the highest ever—over 300,000 a year with 250,000 of these from mothers between 15 and 24. Another 200,000 rushed to the altar for a hasty wedding. An estimated one million had abortions.

One out of every 12 babies born in Oregon is illegitimate. Nationwide, 150,000 girls become pregnant and drop out of school each year. In Chicago alone an average of 700 girls leave public schools each year because of this problem—some as young as ten years old. In New York teachers are taught how to deliver babies that come unexpectedly.

Many unmarried young people use the pill or other contraceptives, but these obviously didn't. These girls didn't expect to have a pregnancy, felt it "unromantic" to plan ahead, tried to get even with a parent, tried to trap the boy into marriage, tried to find love by starting with the end result, or just plain didn't know the facts of life.

Venereal diseases are skyrocketing—this in a time when better treatment and more efficient antibiotics are available. The two major venereal diseases are gonorrhea and syphilis, ranking first and fourth among communicable diseases in the U.S. Both are spread through sex relations with carriers.

Gonorrhea causes painful inflammation of the genito-urinary tract. Over 1,700,000 cases were reported in the year ending June 30, 1970 by the American Social Health Association.

Syphilis, with 70,000 to 80,000 reported cases, is up 8 per cent from the previous year. The ASHA says physicians "report only between 12 and 19 per cent of the infectious syphilis cases they treat and between 11 and 17 per cent of the gonorrhea cases."

Syphilis is especially serious because of its complications. An infected woman may transmit the disease to her fetus. In either adult or baby, syphilis may cause inflammation of the eyes, bones, liver, heart, or central nervous system and result in blindness or insanity.

"Pandemic" is the term now used to describe the spread of syphilis and gonorrhea. This means that the dread VD diseases are occurring across the entire population.

Premarital sex relations growing out of the "new morality" have "greatly increased the number of young people in mental hospitals," according to Dr. Francis J. Braceland, editor of the *American Journal of Psychiatry.* Changes in sexual mores, Dr. Braceland adds, "have imposed stresses on some college women severe enough to cause emotional breakdown."

Sexual promiscuity, according to psychologist Dr. Lofton Hudson, "leads to a kind of superficiality—it just doesn't mean much. I see this in people I counsel —bachelors in their 30's who have been promiscuous through the years. They don't love anybody; they don't know what it means to love. They have loved superficially so long they just can't form a deep attachment and can't feel deeply toward anyone."

Dr. Florence Clotheir, noted physician of Vassar College, sees the same result from a slightly different angle. "We have taught teens that a girl must be beautiful, glamorous, mysterious, sophisticated, and compliant . . . and that a boy must be a devil-may-care who drinks and is very potent and masculine. Perhaps, as a reaction to this artificial mass-media stereotype, youth in its confusion has developed an almost morbid search for identity. . . . In a sex-saturated society, youth finds itself starved for love."

Vassar's physician continues, "Although 19th-century morality may be outdated, it did provide controls which allowed young people more time to grow up and less chance of being prematurely pressured into experiences for which they were unprepared."

Sexual misadventures, both before and after marriage, are causing untold suffering within the social units of violators. Who can assess the heartbreak of children, parents, and others close to those who participate in illicit sex? Sex is inescapably social in consequences.

Psychiatrist Dr. Ralph Greenson of Beverly Hills, California, says that as women are becoming more assertive and demanding in sexual relationships, American males are growing indifferent to sex. Dr. Greenson, clinical professor of psychiatry at the University of California at Los Angeles, calls this "horrifying—a danger to the future of the human race," and adds: "As sexuality diminishes, frustration leads to aggression. Murder and riot become more frequent, as they are today."

Past civilizations that allowed sexual license and other passions to go unchecked have perished. Historian Arnold Toynbee writes, "Of 21 notable civilizations, 19 perished, not from conquest from without, but from decay within." Historian Dr. J. D. Unwin of Cambridge University studied 80 civilizations existing over a period of 4,000 years and concluded that a society must choose between sexual promiscuity and decline, or sexual discipline and creative energy. He writes, "Any human society is free to choose either to display great energy, or to enjoy sexual freedom; the evidence is that they cannot do both for more than one generation."

Hopefully, the pendulum may have begun swinging back. Movie critic Judith Crist has caustically given her views of the sex film, "I Am Curious Yellow." "All they proved," she said, "is that even sex can be made boring. Some things were never meant to be spectator sports."

Russia, after the Bolshevik Revolution, was plunged into anarchy. Traditional sexual mores were trampled underfoot. Today Russia can properly be called "puritanical," perhaps even "repressive." Communist leaders have recognized the danger of uncontrolled sex.

A totalitarian country can impose controls upon its citizens and exact severe penalties for violations, but what can be done in America, where the rights of the individual are championed? More specifically, what can Christians do to show that sex can be both moral and meaningful? We pursue this question in the concluding chapter.

CHAPTER SIX

Sex Can Be Wonderful

The National Sunday School Association's Youth Survey asked 3,000 teenagers what kind of help they would like to receive from their churches. Counsel on sexual problems ranked first among all 21 items. One of three asked for help in this area. In a similar survey by the Lutheran Church, instruction on Christian views of sex, courtship, and marriage ranked first among 40 items.

Youth are asking for sex education. In the past the church was guilty of giving wrong answers or no answers. More recently, the church, with few exceptions, has been guilty of maintaining a discreet silence. A young Canadian at a church conference wailed, "The church has been telling us what not to do for generations; now it won't tell us what to do."

An "official" Southern Baptist survey received answers from only one seventh of the churches queried. A pastor who refused said, "While we are by no means hiding our heads in the sand . . . it is our feeling that the extremely intimate questions you have assembled belong rather in a school or other generally public survey. . . ." Another pastor who declined told his board of deacons, "It is of such an intimate nature that I can't discuss it with you." Such attitudes give the impression that sex is outside the pale of Christian living—even dirty.

A prominent New York neurologist told 350 physicians in St. Louis that teenage girls are now being beguiled by promises of the "new era" of sex without being shown the "small print." Dr. Max Levin charged that girls are "victims of a swindle being perpetrated by advocates of sexual freedom. They are being told that the standards of the past are outmoded, and that henceforth the watchword is freedom. The teenager is told nothing of the cost of sexual freedom, of its threat to her emotional health and well-being.

"Even if venereal disease were abolished and contraceptive methods 100 percent reliable," Dr. Levin added, "premarital chastity would still be in the interests of the young woman. The advocates of the new era are teaching our youngsters a false sense of values."

"In our so-called emancipation from our Puritan past," Dr. Benjamin Spock writes, "I think we have lost our values."

No question—youth and young adults are being sold a false sense of values by radicals and commercializers of sex. *Playboy*, for example, would be going against its best interests to promote Christian values.

Is Sex Education in Schools the Answer?

What about the much-touted sex education in public schools?

Too much too soon, say objectors. Sex education should be geared to the individual child, they think, and this can't be done in a classroom situation. Opponents also emphasize that too many single women are teaching about something that they have no experience in—or shouldn't have. Proponents say most children don't get sex education at home, and therefore the school can help offset false ideas picked up from peers.

The biggest problem relates to the neutral status schools are supposed to maintain in a pluralistic society.

Some school systems have brought values into their sex education. In Evanston, Illinois, teachers refer to "mothers" and "wives," "fathers and "husbands," and not "men" and "women" in discussing sex. In a film-strip, "About Your Life," that is shown to all fifth-grade boys, a narrator states that the reproductive cycle is part of God's "wonderful plan" for the universe. Instructor Mrs. Kay Newby says, "We really want to emphasize the wholesome aspects of sex, and we've been told, in fact, that it's all right to bring God into it." Another instructor, Ronald Thompson, concurs and adds, "Just so long as we don't promote any particular religion."

"You try to stay just with morals," says Mrs. Newby. "But there are also some who want to delve more deeply. Especially when they come from religious homes. So you go into it. 'This is how I understand it,' you tell them. 'But talk to your own parents and minister. If you have no luck with them, come back to us.'"

By trying to put values into sex education, Evanston may be challenged by church and state purists or by parents who desire a strictly neutral stance. Many communities have been torn apart over the issue of sex education in schools by conflict between those who want a neutral stance and those who want religious values inserted. The future is in doubt.

Public colleges and universities have a similar problem. The tragedy is that many teachers follow a stick-to-the-facts philosophy and do not try to teach values which they themselves may hold. Dr. Mary Calderone, a nationally known sex educator, recalls spending an evening with a group of family life specialists. As they talked, she noted that all had deeply committed and meaningful marriages. "Do you make your commitment clear to your students?" she asked. Most said they did not. When she asked why not, they replied that they didn't like to sound "authoritarian."

Home Remedy?

This leaves home and church. Vance Packard asked 878 U.S. students who they felt should set appropriate standards in male-female intimacy. "Parents" received the highest vote—40 per cent with 29 per cent saying "adults," 20 per cent "youthful peers," 6 per cent "schools," and only 5 per cent "churches."

The sad truth is that many parents do not always set standards or even discuss sex with their children. Fifty-two per cent of a group of Southern Baptist youth said they had *never* discussed sex frankly with their parents.

We may as well face the fact that regardless of what the church did in the past, it is no longer possible for Christians to impose their sexual standards upon the community as a whole. Laws will be limited to protecting sexual victims from violence and exploitation and to preserving public decency and good taste. No matter what we try to do by way of prohibitions there will continue to be four sexual standards: permissiveness without affection, permissiveness with affection, sex within marriage, and abstinence.

We can practice and proclaim a Biblical and Christian view of sex to our own families, congregations, and all others whom we can persuade to listen. This will involve open discussion of sex in good taste and without being prudish.

A Time for Honesty

We can begin by admitting that church views on sex in the past have generally been bad news, not the Good News of the Bible. We can recognize that the negative, repressive stance of the church has made many of us so neurotic that we are unable to think rationally about sex, even from a Christian perspective. For example, we see the word "immoral" in a newspaper and automatically think illicit sex. Why don't we think immorality in reference to stealing or assault?

Why do some people limit obscene words to sexual and excretory functions and organs? Why aren't words such as "nigger," "honkey," or "wop" that degrade persons also considered obscene?

Playboy's Anson Mount relates that years ago the magazine received an occasional letter from a preacher saying, "You evil devils, you're leading the young people straight to hell with pictures of naked women." Mount adds, "I've never gotten a letter from a preacher saying, 'You evil devils, you are leading young people straight to hell with your gourmet food articles.'"

Playboy's man has a point we need to accept. We have preached against sexual indiscretions while winking at gluttony.

Exposing Errors

Having admitted our own failures and hangups, we can go on to compare modern perversions of sex (which are really just re-runs of old views) with the Biblical view.

Let's start with the Playboy philosophy. When we see the rakish rabbit with a bow tie that is Playboy's symbol, we immediately think sex, but sex is only part of the Playboy picture. *Playboy* preaches that pleasure is the first purpose of life, that sex is pleasurable and therefore good both in and out of marriage. *Playboy* calls for people to be happy and get the most out of life.

Let's steal the rabbit's thunder and start saying that God meant for us to enjoy life. Jesus said, "I am come that they might have life . . . and have it more abundantly."[1] Self-seeking pleasure is self-defeating. Those who flit from bed to bed will destroy their capacity to enjoy sex in the meaningful, self-giving way which God intended.

Let's pick up the cue from Women's Lib and show

[1]John 10: 10.

how *Playboy* treats women as things to be enjoyed, then discarded. Francis Breisch, Jr., recalls an old couplet that clearly shows the distinction between the sexual drives of men and women.

Hoggamus, higgamus,
Men are polygamous.
Hoggamus higgamus,
Women monogamous.

Women don't like to be used. They want a relationship that gives them lasting value. So do men if they will admit it. The proper order is: Love people and use things, not the reverse.

Instead of hiding sex in a closet and pretending it isn't there, let's put sex in a proper perspective and say that it is more than animal drive as *Playboy* implies. Let's say that sex can be the highest relationship between man and woman when they are committed to one another in a life-sharing marriage.

Let's say that meaning and fulfillment in life comes by building relationships where we live for others and for God.

The "Playboy philosophy" ran under the name of Epicureanism at the time of Christ. Epicurus taught that the chief purpose of man is to achieve happiness by avoiding pain and enjoying pleasure. Nobody remembers Epicurus anymore and the time will come when people will say, "Playboy? What's that?" And, "Hugh Hefner? Who's he?"

Let's tackle also the so-called "new morality" or "situation ethics."

Playboy claims to be in the "situation ethics" camp but really isn't. Theologian William Hamilton, a "situation ethicist," says in referring to Hugh Hefner, "There is love your neighbor and there is knife your buddy. And he honestly chooses the latter. Living for others, selflessness—these may do for the unsophisticated or for some other century, but for the sophisticated 20th century a new faith is required—looking out for Number One."

Let's be fair to the "new morality" and admit that it comes close to the Bible except for one count: it places reason above revelation and allows man to decide what is the most loving thing to do in a difficult situation. It is basically a humanist ethic which puts persons above rigid obedience to law and considers love the only "moral absolute." Whether a certain action is right or wrong depends upon the situation— therefore "situation ethics."

"Whether any form of sex (hetero, homo, or auto) is good or evil depends on whether love is fully served," says Joseph Fletcher.

He cites the following obscure example: A German mother interned in a Russian prison camp during World War II was told that the only way she could be released and returned to her husband and children would be if she could prove herself to be pregnant. The woman weighed the alternatives and asked a friendly guard to impregnate her. She conceived and was sent back to Berlin where she was reunited with her family. Fletcher calls this "sacrificial adultery."

"Situation ethics" does not encourage promiscuity or casual sex. It considers persons and personal relationships to be primary in considering whether or not to engage in extramarital intercourse.

Make Love Now—Cry Later

Many single young people in love have bought the "new morality" and become intimate on the reasoning that in their situation it was the most loving thing to do. Many have found their "situation" changed and have regretted bending the law. For example, a girl wrote Ann Landers that her boyfriend had ditched her after their first sexual experience, saying, "You made me ashamed of myself. I could never marry you after that. I would always wonder if there had been others." And Vance Packard notes this comment from a girl at a private Midwestern university: "I did not regret what I had done at the time. However, after we broke up . . . I felt terrible about it. I always believed that it should be limited to the one man—husband or definitely future husband."

Packard's survey results strike a blow at those who say sex is okay with the person you *plan* to marry. Fifty-three per cent of the girls admitting to be non-virgins said they had been sexually intimate with *more than one man* and over a third said they had had intercourse with "several" or "many" males.

Trial Marriages?

Dr. Margaret Mead, the anthropologist, has come out in favor of trial marriages where a couple would live together and practice birth control for a period, then mutually decide whether or not to enter into a legally binding marriage and have children. Dr. Benjamin Spock, who has been blamed for misadvising a generation of parents on permissiveness, does not endorse this concept but "recognizes . . . the fact that more . . . idealistic, loving people are living together."

Dr. Mead's proposal would supposedly curtail the high divorce rate that leaves so many children to suffer between divided parents. There is no proof that this would result.

Sociologist Robert Bell says: "Factors that make for good sexual adjustment may have little to do with overall marital adjustment." Emotional and mental maturity, affection, commitment to one another, and other adjustments are also involved. It is obviously true that parties who enter into a contract with a commitment to succeed have a better chance of achieving success than those who are uncertain.

The "new morality" comes up short for the Christian because it is not God-centered. The First Commandment, Jesus said, is to love God with all our being. Love your neighbor as yourself is second. On these *two* Commandments, not just the second, "hang all the law and the prophets."[2] And the Lord also said, "If you love me, you will keep my commandments."[3]

The Bible is specific about sex outside of marriage: It is wrong for the persons involved, and it is sin against the Creator of persons. The "new morality" by its very nature must always leave individuals a loophole for applying "love" as they see it. It's doubtful that a young couple, infatuated with one another, parked on a secluded lane, and listening to dreamy music can lift reason above passion. Dr. Sylvanua Duvall, a love and marriage authority, put it straight to a high-level conference of churchmen in Canada: "We must provide guidance for ordinary, decent people who may have a shallow ethical and religious understanding. . . . Love and the law are the two wheels of a two-wheeled cart; if either one is absent, we go around in circles."

A Call for Help

No matter how much guidance is given, there remains the problem of control in an uncontrolled generation that is told in a thousand ways to seek instant gratification. Scientific advance has not resulted in better discipline. Youth and young adults today are pressured in ways their elders never encountered.

Theologian Harvey Cox, writing in *Christianity and Crisis*, aptly assesses these pressures. "They are constantly bombarded—through clothing styles, entertainment, advertising and courtship mores—with perhaps the most skillfully contrived array of erotic stimulants ever amassed. Their sexual fears and fan-

[2]Matthew 22: 36-40.
[3]John 14: 15, *RSV*.

tasies are studied by motivational researchers and then ruthlessly exploited by mass-media hucksters. Elizabeth Taylor's bosom decorates billboards, and throaty songstresses hum their coarse invitations from transistors."

Lambasting the mass media and irresponsible popular idols will not help troubled youth. Sympathetic understanding will make the sexually bombarded generation willing to listen. Acceptance of those who have lost control and have become the victims of hedonism and the "new morality" will help. The tragedy is that a murderer has a better chance of being forgiven in church circles than a sexual transgressor.

Christ at the Controls

Christ promises not only forgiveness but strength to stand against pressures to conform to what "everybody" with normal sex urges is supposed to be doing. To those who have sinned against God, themselves, and loved ones, Christ will make all things new.[4] He will give power to think and act positively and purely. "Whosoever shall call upon the name of the Lord shall be saved."[5]

The Christian's life is "hid with Christ in God."[6] "We know that the man we once were has been crucified with Christ," Paul assured, "for the destruction of the sinful self, so that we may no longer be the slaves of sin."[7]

It is the "sinful self" that is put behind, not the self which includes God-given sexual desires.

"This is the will of God," the apostle said, "that you should be holy: you must abstain from fornication; each one of you must learn to gain mastery over his body, to hallow and honour it, not giving way to lust

[4] II Corinthians 5: 17.
[5] Romans 10: 13.
[6] Colossians 3: 3.
[7] Romans 6: 6, *New English Bible.*

like the pagans who are ignorant of God. . . . For God called us to holiness, not to impurity."[8]

Plea for Purity

Purity is not the punishment for obeying harsh laws, but the reward for a life of commitment—to God who gave us sex and established marriage, to the loved one whom we esteem, and to our own highest ideals. Purity before marriage is building an "affection savings account" to be withdrawn and spent with joy during marriage. It is waiting until "Christmas" to open your presents.

Purity means sex at the right time with the right person. It means loyalty, honesty, devotion, surrender, and the deep joy of loving for the sake of the person loved.

Martin Luther was wrong when he claimed it was impossible to have spiritual feelings on the marriage bed. Temple Gardner, a missionary to Egypt, was much closer to the divine intent when he, while anticipating marriage, wrote, "And when we meet breast to breast, O God, may it be upon Thine own."

Honeymoon for Life

The excitement and joy of sexual intimacy should not end with the honeymoon. This should mark the beginning of a life of adventure in which two lovers build an enduring and fulfilling relationship.

Both husband and wife should strive to keep the sex desire of the other alive and healthy. Their spontaneous hugs and kisses will be the best introduction to sex education their children can receive.

The wife will learn to adapt to her husband, and the husband to his wife. The husband will try to "give his wife the same sort of love that Christ gave to the

[8]I Thessalonians 4: 3-5, 7, *Ibid.*

Church."[9] The Greek word for "love" in this passage is *agapé*, which is love for the sake of the loved one.

Agapé love is beautifully described in I Corinthians 13. It is "patient," "kind," "never boastful nor conceited, nor rude; never selfish, nor quick to take offence." It "keeps no score of wrongs. . . . There is nothing love cannot face; there is no limit to its faith, its hope, and its endurance."[10]

Now add sex appeal and you have a relationship that the angels will envy.

[9]Ephesians 5: 22-25, *Phillips*.
[10]I Corinthians 13: 4-7, *New English Bible*.

BOOKS OF INTEREST

I included so many quotes and statistics in this short study that it seemed best not to include any footnotes other than Bible references. The following books by modern writers were especially helpful, and I recommend them for general study (although readers will, like myself, not accept every conclusion).

Scanzoni, Letha 1968. *Sex and the Single Eye.* Grand Rapids: Zondervan Publishing House.

Mace, David R. 1970. *The Christian Response to the Sexual Revolution.* Nashville: Abingdon Press.

Peale, Norman Vincent 1965. *Sin, Sex and Self-control.* Garden City: Doubleday & Company.

Patai, Raphael 1959. *Sex and Family in the Bible and the Middle East.* Garden City: Dolphin Books, Doubleday & Company, Inc.

Drakeford, John (copyright 1965 by Broadman Press) *Marriage: Duet or Discord?* Grand Rapids: Zondervan Publishing House.

Christian Medical Society 1969. *Birth Control and the Christian, a Protestant Symposium on the Control of Human Reproduction.* Wheaton: Tyndale House.

Packard, Vance 1970. *The Sexual Wilderness.* New York: Pocket Books.

For teenagers I recommend:

Van Buren, Abigail 1959. *Dear Teen-ager.* New York: Bernard Geis Associates.

For family sex education, I suggest a series of paperback booklets obtainable at low cost from the American Medical Association, 535 N. Dearborn, Chicago, Ill. 60610.

Parents' Responsibility, for parents of young children of preschool and early school age. 25c.

A Story About You, for children in grades 4, 5, and 6. 25c.

Finding Yourself, for boys and girls of approximately junior high age. 30c.

Approaching Adulthood, for young people of both sexes of about 16-20 years of age. 40c.

Facts Aren't Enough, for parents and other adults who may need help in sex education for children from preschool through high school. 40c.